Relationship Cleanup

Relationship Cleanup

How to create and maintain a happy, healthy relationship

JEFFREY TITLE; ELISE TITLE

ISBN-10: 1944377328
ISBN-13: 978-1944377328

Table of Contents

Acknowledgments

We built this efficient little guide on the shoulders of our first couples relationship book, LOVING SMART (Warner Books, 1992), our decades of clinical experience helping hundreds of couples find happiness, and most importantly our ever growing font of self knowledge garnered from 50 plus years of our own successful marriage.

Over the past 20 years Jeff's on-going work with couples has been deeply energized through his study of Relational Life Therapy under the mentorship of its founder, Terry Real (and Terry's mentor, Pia Mellody). Jeff is unendingly grateful for Terry's open-hearted sharing of his brilliant structured approach to couples work and his gracious willingness to share all the ingredients of his secret sauce. Lately Elise has also been attending and helping out at Terry's seminars. Many of the specific points we raise RELATIONSHIP CLEANUP come directly from Terry's teaching.

Jeff also wants to thank his mutual support team of Lisa Merlo-Booth (Woman's Empowerment Coach and Relationship Expert – lisamerlo-booth.com) and Dr. Robert Gratton (founder, The Connecticut Center for Intensive Couples Therapy – intensivecouplestherapy.com) for generously offering their loving support and wisdom.

Our children, David Title and Rebecca Schwartz helped us directly with editorial and technical assistance, and through their loving marriages from which we continuously learn new lessons and enhance our lives through their loving circles.

We are most appreciative of the support, guidance and practical advice of our agents at Curtis Brown Ltd., Mathew Waters (who shepherded this project from its inception) and Steven Saltpeter (who is guiding us through the ever evolving publishing world).

Lastly, but definitely not elastly, a special thanks to each of the couples we have worked with over the years whose bravery and candor inspired our own growth and knowledge.

Introduction

For more than four decades Elise and I have been passionately committed to helping couples have respectful, loving long-term relationships. A number of years back we published our first book about helping couples called LOVING SMART: Putting Your Cards on the Table. Elise, a social worker turned prolific writer, and I, a relational psychologist in private practice, have continued to further develop and simplify our teaching model for helping couples be happier together. Our focus is on promoting the healthy attitudes and behaviors that we think are most important for people who want to learn how to do love relationships right and discouraging the negative attitudes and actions that stand in the way of being happy and fulfilled.

During my stint as Director of Group Psychotherapy at the Charles River Counseling Center, in Newton, MA back in the 1970's I began teaching and supervising clinicians in the art and science of group intervention for couples whose relationships were in trouble. At that time I was highly influenced by the work of Carl Whitaker, who was an amazing, highly engaged family systems therapist. Elise, then a licensed Clinical Social Worker, joined in this couples' work at Charles River and in her own practice during the next few decades.

The publication of LOVING SMART made our insights available to a wider audience (as did the accompanying radio and television appearances), stressing methods for understanding and coping with psychological barriers to lasting intimacy. Subsequently I have brought our approach to hundreds of couples, greatly enhanced by my more recent work with Terrance Real through his Relational Life Institute where I am a Certified Relational Life Master Therapist. Over the years our approach to couples' work has moved away from the clinical "what's wrong with you" point of view to a far more practical notion of just which behaviors will help couples do better and exactly which will not.

As we were piecing together our evolving approach into this new manuscript Elise and I became quite taken with the similarities between the meta view of the currently popular tidying up manuals and our own instructions for making relationships work effectively. In each, the premise holds that by taking a few simple steps to clean and tidy up, whether it is your home or your relationship, the improvements will ultimately lead to a happier life.

In the past few years there have been a proliferation of articles, books and manuals about how best to de-clutter and clean up your home. There are even classes where you can get certified as a House Cleaning Technician. Marie Kondo gives a step-by-step approach to de-cluttering in her popular best-selling book, The Life Changing Magic of Tidying Up. In her book Organic Housekeeping, Ellen Sandbeck encourages you to rid your house of toxic air. Jan M. Dougherty provides some laughs along the way as you read her book on how to clean your house called, The Lost Art of House Cleaning: A Clean House is a Happy Home.

Whether these books offer quick simple concepts like how to best fold your underwear for maximum space and neatness or the best methods for cleaning up your entire home, they share the same premise and that is that once you accomplish the task of de-cluttering and cleaning up your home you will be unlikely to go back to your old messy ways and you will experience newfound peace and happiness.

Think of the challenge of tackling a very messy home. It can feel overwhelming. You put it off, you make half-hearted attempts, you manage to finally straighten up a space somewhat only to see it in the same messy state a week or two later. You might even try to laugh it off, stick a magnet on your fridge that declares the best way to have a clean house is to prevent your children and husband from entering.

But most of us ultimately reach a limit. Imagine there's rotting food in your fridge. You can ignore it for just so long. In our home, when one of us sees mold on the food it's clean out time, at last. After we've finally thrown out the rotten stuff and wiped the fridge down it becomes a pleasure again to open the refrigerator door. In general, for us it's a pretty good rule of thumb that when our home is clean and tidy we feel lighter and more contented.

Cleaning up the emotional space that you and your partner share might seem a more abstract enterprise than home care, yet Elise and I will show in this book that the nature of the task is surprisingly similar. When it comes to your relationship you will need to sort through the emotional clutter that has gathered over time and make some serious decisions about what to keep (holding onto the positives) and what to get rid off (eliminating the negatives). The goal is to keep the best and throw away the negative muck that is gumming up the works and causing you and your partner to be unhappy. In short, to have a healthy relationship you will need to clean up your act.

In reviewing the literature on the concept of cleaning up your relationship as a method similar to cleaning up your home, we came upon a few books that touched on the idea but none that intensively focused on the steps to achieving a "cleaner" relationship and why it is so effective. In <u>Mess: One Man's Struggle to Clean Up His House and Act</u>, the author Barry Yourgrau, a man with a serious hoarding problem, makes the strong connection between the need to clean up both his physical and emotional space and being able to have a successful relationship. While there are also other books that focus on the negative effects on an intimate relationship when one or both partners are "packrats," the premise of our book is to help even the most fastidious couples to understand that hoarded ill feelings and unattended emotional mess will undermine the benefits of even the tidiest homes.

The impact of the similarities between cleaning up homes and cleaning up relationships came into striking relief a few months back when Elise and I decided to pare down many years worth of accumulated stuff in preparation for the downsizing that an upcoming move to New York City would inevitably entail. We not only had to face the stuff in plain view but all the many cupboards, file cabinets, closets and taped up cardboard boxes we'd managed to avoid dealing with for years. Every so often we'd talked about going through some of those hidden away places only to quickly go on to doing something less stressful – exemplifying the old adage of putting off today what you can do tomorrow. Well, now, tomorrow had finally come.

Taking guidance from the de-cluttering movement, our strategy was first to go room-by-room sorting through everything in plain view, making our way eventually down to the bottom of the piles. The deeper we got the tougher the process. The challenge got harder when we began opening overstuffed drawers, files, closets, revealing an amazing amount of stuff that we'd forgotten all about. Our questions were similar to ones we had read about other people asking. What had we been saving it all for? What could we let go of? What did we want to keep? What kind of value did we place on things we were reluctant to toss?

We couldn't help feeling abashed at how much clutter and detritus had accumulated beneath our radar—so like the emotional clutter that quickly accumulates when couples minimize their problems and fail to creatively address their negative feelings. This was the beginning of our continuing conversation about the similarity between the "neat" movement's way of approaching household order and our emerging framework for making intimate relationships lasting and loving.

Elise and I came together as teenagers—inexperienced, insecure and desperate to find happiness together. Our raw teenage emotions were so close to the surface that pushing them under the rug was not yet an option. And living under the sway of ginned up negative emotions was unbearable. We were fortunate to realize early on in our relationship that the longer we let a negative feeling hold sway the more we suffered. Shortly, we both went for extensive graduate school training and became even more sensitized to the need to be positive and supportive as our marriage continued. Helping hundreds of couples over the decades greatly helped inspire us to pay attention to our love for each other and keep working to make ourselves happy together. Fifty plus years later we've distilled the personal and professional wisdom we acquired along the way into simple and accessible lessons to train and inspire couples everywhere to seek a happier future together. These lessons have been successful for us and successful for the many couples with whom we've both worked. With a little practice and a lot of determination we believe it will work for you. The goal here is simple—to achieve a happier, more loving relationship.

We have broken down our book into two parts. In Part One, we focus on which missteps most damage intimate relationships and why. These are our Relationship Don'ts and besides listing and describing what they are we share what we think you should do about them. In this section we explore:

How relationships get so unhealthy in the first place.

How holding on to negative feelings can make you emotionally and physically ill.

How the unhealthy approaches couples too often undertake to make the relationship better only make matters worse.

We also take a step back to encourage you to reflect on what your relationship was like when you first fell in love. During the height of your romance you may have felt the perfect connection and you were walking on cloud nine. But once you came down to earth you were likely to discover your love relationship had become messier than it seemed when you were floating up there in the sky.

Conflicts arise in all developing and ongoing intimate relationships and produce negative emotions like anger, confusion and disappointment. Hoarded, they begin the dirty work of eroding your love. With amazing speed these negative feelings can occupy so much of an expanse in your hearts and minds that there is little space left for positive feelings to thrive.

Much like the task of cleaning up your home, the need to clean up your relationship may go unnoticed for some time. You have to see the *dirt*, something you tend to ignore as much as possible until the mess threatens to overwhelm you. One aim we have in this book is to help you deal with the emotional debris before it gets so bad you need the help of a professional—a kind of mental health cleaning service to tackle the overspill.

You will likely recognize and even be all too familiar with some of the negative behaviors presented in Part One. Maybe you've done them yourself or learned to accept them from your partner (or at least tell yourself you accept them). We believe that bad behavior is learned and that it can be unlearned, replaced instead with behaviors that are positive and keep the relationship clean and polished. And this leads us to Part Two of Relationship Cleanup.

In Part Two, we move on from Relationship Don'ts to present a series of positive steps to make your interactions better right away, followed by a program of emotional de-cluttering to lighten the long-term maintenance load. These are your tools for creating the best environment for sustaining a long-term healthy relationship. This section is all about Relationship Do's. We focus on building up goodwill for maximum relationship resilience, and show you how you can create the best conditions for long term intimacy to flourish. By practicing these quick-start approaches you will create greater trust and intimacy that, in turn, makes it less threatening to dig deeper and fully clean up your act.

Neither Elise nor I can recall any examples from our work or personal lives, of people who didn't want to be happy, or happier, in their intimate relationships. If not the top priority on their list of wants and needs, it is usually pretty close to the top. In life, there are so many challenges, stresses, disappointments and losses. Being in a happy intimate relationship gives you someone you love with whom to share those burdens. And in times of joy and success, you have a partner who can truly celebrate with you.

Current research supports our intuitive belief in the desire for and benefits of happiness in intimate relationships. For instance, The Harvard Study of Adult Development, begun in 1938, has been following the lives of a number of Harvard University men as well as a group of young men from inner city tenements. One of their primary conclusions was this – "Good relationships keep us happier and healthier. Period." (Robert Waddinger, Ted Talks Posted on internet December 2015)

Wanting your relationship to be positive and fulfilling may be a given, but many couples lack the skills to reach that goal. The relationship cleanup we're recommending will take commitment and work. The payoff—like the results of the right kind of house cleaning—is a deep sense of peace and joy. By first following our quick easy tips then moving on to a deeper cleaning you will experience the many benefits of good relationship practices. You will learn new ways to deepen your closeness, enhance your enjoyment of each other and find the happiness you want in your intimate relationship.

Let's get started.

Part One
Bad Cleanup

In The Weeds
When someone becomes overwhelmed and falls behind.

Chapter One
How did our relationship get so messy?

In Part ONE we want to begin by exploring when the bad habits developed and began to clutter up your relationship. Our guess is you probably didn't even know it was happening at first. Or at least, it's unlikely you anticipated the way the overlooked issues would mount up. Realizing how problems develop and take hold in relationships is vital to understanding how you got into the mess you find yourselves in now as well as to prevent the establishment of new messes.

To answer the question about when things began to get messy between you—let's reflect back to all the decisions you made early on and how you made them. New couples need time to develop negotiating skills but time is not on their side. Think first about your individual differences and tastes and how they impacted on your partner. These could seem quite minor—I like quiet when I go to sleep, my partner needs the TV on: I like bright colors, my partner is all about beige: I like to socialize with friends on the weekend, my partner likes to hang around the house: I like ocean vacations, my partner prefers the mountains: I like bluegrass, my partner likes classical.

The list usually goes on and on. It's not the differences in themselves that ultimately create a messy build-up of anger, resentment and frustration, it's how you as a couple handle and negotiate differences.

Differing interests and styles can affect your expectations and accumulate disappointments. In your effort to make everything emotionally tidy when you first fall in love, you may excuse, ignore or deny potentially troubling issues.

And we're not saying all differences cause problems. Everyone knows that opposites attract. It's certainly true that differences can add excitement and vitality to a blossoming relationship. You can each learn from the other and expand your own horizons. True appreciation and loving accommodation are relational assets.

Differences become clutter when they bother, frustrate or annoy you but you ignore them on the one extreme or harp on every difference at the other. In either case you're not going to clean up the mess, you're just leaving room for much more to accumulate.

When the mess slowly gathers over time you may be unaware of it or let it slide until one day you finally get a clear picture of the heap of detritus piled up all around you and you know you're in trouble. Some couples' perceived differences cause almost immediate friction. Newly committed couples who find themselves buried in conflict rarely know what to tackle first and how to tackle it. We advise dealing with your relational difficulties as early and often as possible.

We liken the explosion of early relational conflicts to the big city grime that oozes constantly into our son and daughter-in-law's street level apartment. If they ignored it even for a day, they'd find a layer of soot on everything they touched. To keep the place livable, my daughter-in-law says that she has to dust and vacuum three times or more a day. In effect, she's taking a proactive and health conscious approach to the problem. Unfortunately when some couples have intense conflicts and lack the good habit of cleaning up their emotional conflicts frequently enough they can be buried in detritus scarily fast. Failure to clean up emotional mess, whether it came on fast or slow, creates a breeding ground for sustained bad feelings.

While they were courting Mary and Carl were aware that they had different spending habits. They sometimes argued about their dissimilar feelings about money but the arguments were brief and quickly dismissed by both as minor. They believed the dust settled after each unresolved spat and didn't cause either of them further distress. But after nearly twenty years of marriage the couple is practically at war over what Carl sees as Mary's shopping addiction and what Mary sees as Carl's tightwad personality.

Reflecting back they admit that the first incident, that bothered them both more than either would admit, happened when they got engaged. Mary wanted a particular diamond engagement ring and Carl thought it way too expensive. She let it go but she was already thinking Carl was tightfisted. And Carl worried that Mary was too cavalier about money. When they married and Mary began choosing furnishings for their first apartment they argued over cost and the issue of necessity over desire. Mary would become pouty and negative and Carl became withdrawn.

Neither Mary nor Carl were able to cope with this serious difference between them nor were either of them able to confront the problem with the other and try to work out a satisfactory compromise. Matters got worse and an unhealthy pattern developed. Mary spent more, Carl became more tightfisted and their constant arguing finally brought them into my office.

During an early visit Mary complained that Carl was so cheap he wouldn't even buy himself a new pair of shoes even though they were so worn out there were holes in the soles. For emphasis she grabbed a shoe off Carl's foot to show me. The sole was worn thin but no hole—yet. In retaliation, the next week Carl pulled out the previous month's credit card statement to show me how much Mary had spent on purchases for herself and the house. Most assuredly this was a couple in a big mess. They desperately needed lessons in how to cleanup this problem.

Now take our friends Ron and Alice. They, too, had serious financial differences—with a twist. Unlike Carl, Ron had no trouble spending money—on himself. The stinginess came when his wife Alice wanted something for herself or the house. Ron would say it wasn't necessary and Ron was the breadwinner and held the purse strings. One day, forty plus years into their marriage Alice thought she would shame Ron by holding a tag sale and selling a bunch of stuff in their house. Elise went to the tag sale. There was a beautiful and very expensive men's sweater that Elise admired—the tag was still attached—and Alice insisted on selling it to her for $10, telling her Ron never liked it. Fast forward a few months. Elise and I are at a gathering and I'm wearing this gorgeous sweater when who should walk over to us but Ron and Alice. Immediately Ron says to me, "Hey, I have that sweater, too." And Alice replies nonchalantly, "Not anymore."

Karen and Gene argue about sex. Karen feels Gene is too sexually demanding and Gene worries that Karen is frigid. While they had more sex in the early years Karen admits she never wanted sex as frequently as Gene did although she never told him that. Now, with children, work, other responsibilities she thinks it's natural that she wants less sex. She's often too tired or stressed to feel romantic. Gene thinks Karen would really prefer not having sex at all. Both Karen and Gene admit they knew that sex was a potentially troubling issue that they should have tried to work out earlier but in this situation the build-up of the problem seemed easier for them to dismiss than to, as they put it, make waves.

Elise and I had issues over chores that we failed to deal with head-on in the early years of our marriage. I was pretty sloppy while Elise liked things clean and tidy. Though she did complain at times she usually "resolved" her problem by doing much of the clean up on her own. Then there was the matter of washing the dishes. Okay, I could see that she did more than her fair share of chores so I agreed I would wash, dry and put away the dinner dishes—no dishwasher back then. I thought I was handling this chore quite well although there were times I was too wiped at night and I'd leave the dirty dishes in the sink until morning. If Elise showed disapproval I would childishly remind her there was no imposed time limit as long as I got my chore done.

In a way we were lucky that less than a few months into our marriage (several years into our relationship), our apartment in a Brooklyn brownstone became infested with roaches. When Elise found them feasting on the prior night's dirty dishes she was ready to do battle. I was defensive at first then argued that she was getting overly dramatic. But I knew I didn't have a leg to stand on. What also happened—and this is so common— was that other gripes she had with me and that I had with her poured out. How quickly we'd gone from hot headed teens who just had to voice their feelings to young adults with emotional filters and repressed anger breaking out under pressure. When that happens we're really just flinging dirt around. It was only after we both made a determined effort to focus on the issue at hand that we resolved the dirty dishes in the sink problem. I washed them right after dinner from that time on to this day. And Elise loves going to bed at night and seeing a spotless kitchen. I've come to like it too.

Differences that can cause problems down the line don't have to be around the big issues of finances, sex or chores. For Gayle and Alan, the dust they ignored started over a gift Alan gave Gayle for their one-month anniversary—they're now married close to six years—a highly protective case for her iPhone, which he thought was useful and practical. And the very fact that he gave her something to acknowledge their first month of marriage he viewed as romantic. Gayle, on the other hand, was perfectly happy with her old case. And she felt that if Alan were going to celebrate this mini-anniversary, she would have much preferred a more intimate gift—something personal, even frivolous. But she took this gift faux pas as a small disappointment and told herself it was no big deal. Alan says he had no idea she was disappointed, but he admits that as the years have gone by she's complained during some altercation or other that he is never romantic and would it kill him to surprise her with a bunch of flowers on her birthday?

In any intimate relationship it's easy at first to let some clutter gather. But when you begin mentally lumping together all the little spats and letdowns into a "forget about it" bucket, that bucket can fill up rapidly and soon you are looking at the burgeoning contents of your "can't forget about it" trash can.

Ignoring or making excuses works for some couples up to a point. Denial and rationalization are the handy tools of those who don't want to face a cleanup. But the mess doesn't vanish—it just hides out. Even if one of you might successfully overlook the mounting clutter, chances are at some point the other will begin to find it a problem.

When Elise was a teenager her mom would make her vacuum her room. As soon as she finished the chore her mom would march in and immediately lift up the corner of the shaggy green rug, revealing a film of dust and a slip of paper or two. "But mom," Elise would complain, "who looks under the rug?" Her mom's reply: "Dirt is dirt, whether you can see it or not. The room is not really clean if it isn't clean everywhere." A little extreme, but definitely close to the mark.

In our many years of treating couples, Elise and I frequently encountered clients whose habit was to regularly hide a lot of dirt under the rug. Their philosophy was the same as Elise's was as a teen about her room. If you don't see it you don't have to deal with it.

You know your relationship has gone off the rails when disappointment, anger frustration, sadness, and regret have built up over time until now they are prominent in your relationship. These troubled feelings make you stressed and unhappy. While you may think by letting this problem or that one slide it will dissolve over time, it's really another messy piece of business that joins all the others under the rug. When you finally lift up that rug, don't be surprised when the dust goes flying! Emotional clutter has a way of accumulating over the years and can ultimately suffocate your relationship.

Chapter Two
Mess = Stress = Getting Sick

A modicum of common sense tells you that unhappy relationships are very stressful. This stress is, unsurprisingly, quite likely to be unhealthy. Many studies have shown the strong connection between stress and poor health. In a June 2014 article written for WebMD entitled "The Effects of Stress on your body" the summary conclusion was that "Stress can play a part in problems such as headaches, high blood pressure, diabetes, skin conditions, asthma, arthritis, depression, and anxiety." (sourced from NIMH, American Heart Association and Mayo Clinic.)

Lisa Jaremka, a postdoctoral fellow at Ohio State University's Institute for Behavioral Medicine Research, did a study showing that individuals anxious about their intimate relationships "had higher levels of the stress hormone cortisol, and lower levels of T-cells, which are important in the immune system to fight off infections." The study found "a link or association between relationship anxiety and the body's stress and immune response" although the study did not "prove cause and effect". (WebMD-"Relationship Worries Can Make You Sick)

Google marital stress and physical illness and you'll come up with a slew of links. Some link to experientially based blogs and stories, others to the results of scientific studies. The general consensus is that a bad marriage or long term relationship can make you physically ill. A number of studies found that continual strife in a long-term relationship negatively effect cardiovascular health. Studies show the link between stress and high blood pressure and higher cholesterol level. Women unhappy in their relationships seem particularly prone to increased risk factors in heart disease. Studies also point to the links between stress and type two diabetes, because of increased blood glucose levels. The direct correlation is between relationship stress and bad health, but it is often the case that people feeling stress don't exercise enough or eat well. When you're unhappy in your relationship for prolonged periods of time you feel drained of the kind of energy needed to take good care of yourself. It might lead to negative, even harmful habits—drinking too much, eating too much, smoking, taking drugs—in attempts to alleviate the emotional stress you are feeling. Ultimately you become both emotionally and physically sicker. All this to say now is the time to constructively deal with the stress generated from an unhealthy relationship.

Vanessa and Emily came for help because of constant arguments that were, as they described, stressing them both out. Vanessa was having trouble sleeping and was overeating, Emily complained of being unable to concentrate at work and had begun picking fights with some of her friends. When I asked what they argued about, they said, practically in unison, "everything." In effect, their relationship had become toxic. And the stress was becoming unbearable. Emily told Vanessa that if she ended up having a heart attack it would be Vanessa's fault. That caused a fierce argument in the office, Vanessa accusing Emily of being a drama queen, Emily accusing her partner of being cold and uncaring. As if to prove her wrong, Vanessa started to cry and said she didn't know how much more of this she could take. They agreed that if this help didn't work, they would have to split up. I congratulated them, as I have congratulated many others, on making the courageous choice of acknowledging the seriousness of their problems in a safe forum where we could begin to find a better way.

Karen and Peter first came to see me as a couple on the verge of divorce. At least Karen was standing on that precipice. The couple had been married for close to seven years and Karen had pretty near reached her limit. She told Peter that if he didn't agree to therapy she was leaving him. Peter was a reluctant patient. He didn't want a divorce but he was quick to minimize their problems, at least any of the problems that Karen felt he contributed to or was even responsible for. Peter told me he was there to help his wife. The way he saw it, Karen had blown everything wrong in their relationship totally out of proportion. The real problem, as he saw it, was Karen. He claimed she was prone to depression and was hot-tempered. Was it any wonder, she was on meds for high blood pressure and was plagued by skin rashes that her dermatologist connected to stress. Peter thought Karen needed to work on herself and he was willing to help any way he could.

Karen became enraged with her husband's attitude. But I zeroed in on Peter's offer to help. What exactly was he willing to do? Would he be willing to behave differently in certain situations that upset Karen? Would he address any of his habits that added stress to the relationship? No? After several more questions in that vein, all three of us began to consider the possibility that Peter was reluctant to consider his role in their relationship problems.

Peter came for two more couple's sessions then dropped out. Karen continued to see me. After a few months she felt strong enough and confident enough to leave Peter and file for a divorce. Within days of making the break, Karen reported feeling relieved, and while she still experienced stress about being on her own, she was getting in touch with new feelings of anticipation and excitement. She had opened a door. Looking back she saw that she'd paid a big emotional price for tolerating Peter's refusal to be accountable. With my encouragement, she sought out friends and family who were supportive and positive. A month after separating, Karen told me her rashes were healing. She said she felt emotionally and physically better. She came to understand that stress in and of itself is something everyone experiences and has to deal with. But the stress that had come from an unhappy, unhealthy relationship felt endless and overwhelming. Granted, the emotional and physical change in Karen is purely anecdotal but I'm using her as an example of many patients that I've treated who experienced similar improvements from reductions in relational stress. Ideally, as the result of relational progress, but that is not always possible.

All intimate relationships, no matter how new or long lasting, require an endless series of negotiations, decision-making, compromises, resolving conflicting values, combining or accommodating differing personal and cultural expectations, differences of opinion, differing problem-solving styles—on an almost daily basis. Many of these relational challenges prove difficult to smooth out successfully. But at least the stress abates when the problem gets dealt with fairly, instead of lingering and festering. When it is left to fester, when a couple isn't willing to accept mutual responsibility and tackle the mess together, the stress becomes an overbearing burden.

Not only does a problem-filled relationship cause stress, the stress itself can so preoccupy you that you find yourself missing doctor or dentist appointments, not paying attention to health issues that crop up for whatever reason. In short, you stop taking care of yourself. These direct and secondary effects of feeling so much stress may, over time, make you more susceptible to acute or chronic health issues.

Having a healthy satisfying intimate relationship won't solve all the other causes of stress in your lives. There will still be anxiety about work, money, children, in-laws, ageing parents. Elise and I know this very well. But we also know from long personal and professional experience that when you are happy together as a couple you form a winning team. You can help each other cope with outside stresses. You have someone you trust who you can turn to for support, understanding, and help when you need it. In short, you have each other's back. That is an incredibly comforting feeling and that alone can temper many of the stresses you will undoubtedly face.

Chapter Three
Messes made worse

Couples aren't just sitting around settling for being miserable in their relationships, accepting high levels of stress, making no effort to improve their situation. People try to make things better and they honestly are doing the best they can. Unfortunately many of their intuitive strategies inadvertently make things worse. In our many years of working with unhappy couples we have witnessed these efforts and the destructive, frequently disastrous results they produce. All too often people haven't a clue as to what they are doing wrong.

Old bad habits keep your relationship cluttered, especially when you aren't even aware you've got them. However, in order to adapt new healthy relationship habits it's important to recognize what you're doing wrong and why it's not producing the positive results you want. If you understand *why* these approaches are actually making your marriage worse, you'll have extra motivation for change. Keep doing it wrong and you'll never get things right between you. Stop inflicting pain and mess on your previously precious relationship and maybe it won't be too late to turn things around.

Terrance Real, Founder of the Relational Life Institute, author of several excellent books on relationships, and one of my most influential mentors, has done a great job identifying the primary ways that couples typically stumble, which he calls "failed strategies." I have been studying with Terry for several years, and have applied many of his ideas and concepts both professionally and personally. As we both see it people are trying all the time to heal their disharmony, but instinctively choose tactics that only make things worse. The harder they try the wrong things, the bigger the mess they create. Frustrated, angry, despairing they go at it again. If you have ever been in a love relationship of any length of time some of these failed techniques will sound dismayingly familiar. Don't despair. We have all fallen into one or another of these traps from time to time. Elise and I still slip into them on occasion and have to catch ourselves before we end up creating a mess.

So what are couples attempting over and over that will never work?

Trap 1: You stop the conversation to correct the veracity of a statement your partner has made.

It can be something minor like:

Ben "I caught a 20 lb. bass yesterday."

Gloria "Please, it was closer to 10 lbs."

Ben - "Right, like you know. You were busy puking over the side of the boat. Gloria - "I saw that fish. It looked malnourished."

Ben - "She doesn't know what she's talking about. She never caught a fish in her life. I saw the scale. Admit it, Gloria, you never saw what it weighed."

And the conversation about the day they went fishing got flushed down the rabbit hole of who is the one telling the truth. Frustrated by their differences they press their points until one or the other gives in, starts a fight, or withdraws. This is never a path to closeness.

I fall into this problem behavior all too often. Elise is discussing an issue of hers and I feel compelled to challenge a point she's made I don't think is factual. Maybe some demented part of my mind thinks she'll feel better if she has all her facts straight. For that split second I'm fulfilling some inner need to take on the role of the good judge. But there are no good judges among intimates. At that moment I'm convinced it's my sacred job to keep the facts straight, when what's really crucial is helping Elise express and explore her feelings. Far from being some sort of hero here I've gone far to create distance and hard feelings.

Recently, Elise was telling me about the cardio support group she mentors and I proceeded to question her belief that support groups really work. Before she responded I started spouting statistics and information I'd gleaned from articles supporting my point that they aren't really effective. Elise who is very aware of my "search for truth" hang-up started to get angry at me for misdirecting her conversation but opted for a more effective tack. "You don't get it. I'm looking for understanding and support, here, not facts and statistics." I was reminded as too often in the past, that getting caught up in proving my truth or disproving Elise's is a serious distraction from exploring her truth, which is what was actually the relational business at hand. This is a basic tenant of Relational Life Therapy—*you can be right or you can be married.*

Trap 2: You try to get your way via manipulation. Even if your manipulations succeed, your relationship becomes lopsided, unequal. It is near impossible to be in a sharing give-and-take relationship if one partner is the controller and the other the controlee. When you control through manipulation you again believe you are the one in the right. You tell yourself you are acting out of love. You feel righteous, justified. But your partner feels denigrated, disrespected and ultimately resentful. And resentfulness breeds poor relationship health.

Trap 3. Terrance Real calls this trap "unbridled self-expression." When you use sharing "your truth" as a tool for hurting your partner. It often starts with "I'm just being honest here," or "If you want to know the truth...," or "This has really been bugging me and I just have to tell you..." These sentences often finish with criticisms that are invariably less than subtle. "You really need to lose a few pounds." Or "You really embarrassed yourself at that party last night." Or "You really got a lousy haircut this time." It goes on and on.

Sounds unbelievably insensitive. But as a relational therapist, I've witnessed just such insensitivity and thoughtlessness time and time again. "I have to say this even if it hurts you." And the logic? The justification? "We each have to be honest with the other." The justification goes further. "Even if I hurt you now, in the end you will "see the light" and change your ways."

When has that ever happened? Never! When you are on the receiving end of a sharp, cruel critique, especially when the attack comes from your loved one, your hurt feelings do just the opposite of making us more pliable. Your pain grows and turns to anger, both emotions that make feeling loving just about impossible. And your partner is frustrated and feels hopeless about anything ever changing. Who wins? No one. The fact is negative actions lead to negative reactions.

Trap 4: Getting even. There seems to be a natural justice here; you mess up my half of the closet so I'll trash your side. But the more you deliberately make your partner pay for a perceived hurt, the more you have a hurting partner and the less you have to love. And when your loved one gives as good as they get the fights escalate. They get downright ugly. Finally, you are at war. This is how to turn a mess into your own personal garbage dump.

Trap 5. This is the great disappearing act. Here, you end up dealing with relationship problems through emotional and/or physical withdrawal. In effect, you create an impenetrable wall of distance. That distance will disempower your partner. You simply cannot solve mutual problems while you are all alone. Some of you may rationalize your silence by telling yourself your partner already has so much on their plate and/or what you're feeling isn't all that important in comparison. When you get into this mind-set all you do is diminish your feelings and in so doing devalue them.

So many hurts, frustrations and anger lead to emotional hoarding. It starts small and forms a stockpile over time. Just as packrats and serious hoarders let stuff pile up and refuse to look at why they are holding onto so many things, so too do emotional hoarders. The mess keeps growing and soon you are trapped in a mountain of emotional debris and you cannot see a way out from the weight. It can become suffocating, dangerously unhealthy.

Hoarders often cling to material items because the objects they save impart meaning and safety to their lives. Each and every one of their hoarded possessions is absolutely necessary for their sense of wellbeing. They overlook the dirt, the mold, fire hazards. So too do emotional hoarders focus on the need to feel safe. They think that by holding onto their feelings they will avoid ugly arguments and resulting emotional injury. They fear the fight. The solution isn't for them to swallow their feelings or bundle them up and hide them away—it's learning how to fight fairly and trusting your partner to work towards the same.

Whatever your rationalizations, the reality is that keeping your feelings hidden away is an effective act of aggression. By withholding feelings you are actually striking out by being dismissive. You are dismissing your partner as not worthy of your time, consideration or involvement. By acting this way you are discrediting your investment in the relationship. And don't think for a moment that your hoarding goes unnoticed. It can be the worst sort of emotional clutter observed by loved ones who cannot find a way to break through the mess to which you are clinging.

When hoarding is employed as a technique in your relationship it is a disaster. It can bleed into all the other unsuccessful techniques discussed above. It can spark retaliation—the more you hoard, the more your partner may feel justified in unbridled expression of their feelings. Or your partner can also withdraw so now you're both into a hoarding mode. In either instance, you've reached a stalemate. Nothing gets cleaned up.

So many losing strategies. So many disengaged, unhappy couples. Not only do these overused failed approaches never clean up the mess, they generate even more mess that in turn leads to increased stress and diminished happiness in your love life.

If you let your feelings spill all over the place; if you withdraw because the mess is too much for you; if you harbor resentment, frustration, anger; if you attack the problem of mess thoughtlessly; if you become controlling or vindictive; if you and/or your partner use any or all of these wasteful approaches—you will find yourselves trapped in a negative cycle. Doing all the wrong things for what you've told yourself are for all the right reasons is clearly not the answer. A clean and shiny relationship is promoted by doing as many of the right things as you can while steering clear of behavior that only makes things worse. And isn't a big part of life about learning right from wrong?

Chapter Four
Grudges - The Dirt You Don't See

Every intimate relationship creates endless invitations for forming grudges. Grudges have the powerful potential of turning your lover into your enemy. A recent quote from Pope Francis beautifully describes the situation:

"There is no perfect family. We don't have perfect parents, we are not perfect, we don't get married with a perfect person nor do we have perfect kids. We have complaints of each other. We were disappointed with each other. Therefore, there is no healthy marriage or healthy family without the exercise of forgiveness. Forgiveness is vital to our emotional health and spiritual survival. Without forgiveness the family becomes a theatre of conflict and a bastion of grievances. Without forgiveness the family gets sick. Forgiveness is the sterilization of the soul, the cleaning of the mind and the liberation of the heart... Who does not forgive sickens physically, emotionally and spiritually. That's why the family has to be a place of life and not of death; territory of healing and not of disease; stage of forgiveness and not of guilt. Forgiveness brings joy where sorrow produced pain; and healing, where pain caused disease."
From Vancouver Diocesan CWL

To create an enduring relationship you need to start out immediately separating the little differences from the incidents that stick in your craw.

Master the art of letting go of small hurts and disappointments with good grace and all of the acceptance you can muster. Engage the remaining issues as soon as possible and pride yourself in accepting less than perfect solutions, because none of us is perfect.

The heart of this approach is to minimize the accumulation of hard feelings. If you are both all over this one from the start you will be way ahead of the game. Unfortunately, grudge accumulation can be stealthy and take on a life of its own. Imagine those grudges as a huge pile of detritus that has collected in your home over the years. Do you ignore it? Close your eyes so you can't see the mess? Simply let it fester until it's so bad you can't deal with it at all?

Whenever you feel your partner has done or said something egregious, hurtful, thoughtless, and dismissive and you don't try to clean up the spill when it happens, a grudge insidiously forms in your mind. Grudges start early and they may start small. You may not realize at first that you are tracking the times your partner does or says something that upsets you that you can't just shake off and aren't able to resolve when it happens. Instead the hurt or anger you feel gets lodged in your mind as a grudge. The more things like this happen the more grudges are collected and stored away. They pile up and take occupancy in your head. It's not that you're constantly thinking about this grudge or that, but the distressing feelings they arouse can pop up at any time, often when you least expect it. When they do, you relive the old hurt. With no real sense of the problems you are causing yourself your mind becomes stuck in a grievance loop.

Lets focus on a particular grudge, one that is typical of many grudges you might hold against your partner. Meet my friend Bill whose wife forgot his birthday a few years back. It felt like every time anyone had a birthday gathering he would bring this up. He might get a moment of pleasure from relating her offense but the feelings generated in him were mainly hurt and anger. And it didn't matter that his wife apologized and never again forgot his birthday. Actually, she had long gotten used to his remarks about her failure and they no longer had the desired guilt effect on her. Bill was left having all the upset feelings that this memory engendered. He was the one holding on to the resentment, keeping the grievance alive. He felt righteous in holding this grudge, thinking that his wife deserved it. But who was really being punished here? Who was the one suffering?

Nelson Mandela framed the issue elegantly: "Resentment is like drinking poison and waiting for your enemy to die." Resentment hurts the grudge holder most of all."

Why was it that Bill could not let go of this grudge? Why was this one forgetful moment on his wife's part so terrible that he couldn't drop it? When he and Paula first fell madly in love, Bill never imagined his beloved would do anything that would hurt or disappoint him. Even if she slipped up a little he was still in a romantic haze and was able to let it slide because there was so much trust between them, so strong a feeling of being loved and understood. And as long as Bill felt that for the most part he was getting what he wanted he didn't have to question whether or not any of his expectations were realistic.

Inevitably, the romantic haze lifted and now when some word or deed on Paula's part disappointed him it was not so easy for him to write it off. At first he was baffled. Why was Paula breaking the trust that had been so strong between them? Why was she disappointing him, why was she no longer meeting his expectations?

By the time Paula forgot his birthday, more than twenty years after they married, Bill was already harboring a number of grudges against Paula for what he viewed as infractions of their trust. At this point he was feeling wary, guarded, and ready to take offense each time Paula disappointed him. The partner who once could do no wrong was now doing plenty wrong. Every time this happened Bill found he was no longer minimizing the offence, he was maximizing the impact it had on him. He went from thinking "no big deal" to "this is unforgivable."

When Paula forgot his birthday that day it was almost as if Bill was just waiting for that next offense as if to prove that he was justified in holding on to his grudges. Bill felt righteous in hoarding all his grudges against Paula. He held on to them as a form of self-protection, as if the grudges would somehow keep him from getting hurt again. Ironically, it was the grudges themselves that were hurting him. Carrying that kind of burden brings with it a slew of negative effects. Whenever Bill relived a hurt or disappointment he relived the feelings that accompanied the original insult. He felt unhappy all over again. His stress level would go up, his blood pressure would rise, he suffered headaches and stomach aches. Too much stress, as you read earlier, is a factor that can lead to more serious health complications.

Grudges also create walls that keep you apart from your partner, and sour the opportunity for creating and sharing good feelings because you can no longer see over your mountain of resentments. Bill's grudges meant that he had less space in his heart and mind for experiencing positive loving feelings with Paula. Bill loved Paula and they both wanted to be in a loving, nurturing, healthy relationship. As long as Bill held on to his grudges they couldn't move forward. But grudges are tenaciousness. How do they get so powerful?

Let's stick with the example of Paula forgetting Bill's birthday. On that day Bill felt hurt and disappointed. Did he tell her? No. He decided it was his wife's responsibility to remember, not his responsibility to remind her. And he took some small measure of pleasure knowing that when she did finally remember she would feel guilty. And he wanted her to feel guilty. He wanted her to suffer too. So, the next day she did remember and apologized. She wanted to celebrate that night, but Bill was not receptive. In his mind, it would have meant giving her a pass. So what happened? He began to build this incident up, like so many others, as something more serious. If she could forget my birthday what else will she forget? Does a loving wife really forget her husband's birthday? Is she less loving than I once believed? I feel less trusting now. I don't even think she was really all that sorry. She has even teased me about it. I find that particularly insensitive. And I saw how she fawned over my friend Joe at his birthday last year. Maybe there's something going on that I don't know about...

All these thoughts cascaded in his mind but here's some things Bill wasn't even considering. Was his wife preoccupied the day of his birthday because maybe one of the children was sick, or was there something happening at work that was pressing on her mind? Was she feeling well? Was her act of forgetfulness part of a serious pattern or was it unrealistic of Bill to expect his wife would never slip up when it came to him?

By not dealing with the relational problem and at the same time hoarding his hurt, he was left reliving it over and over again and without realizing it, the offense was taking on broader and more powerful meaning.

Remember the old game of "Telephone". You'd sit around in a circle with a group of people and the first person would whisper something in his partner's ear who in turn would try to repeat it and this would continue until you came to the last person who would then say aloud what he heard. It's never exactly or often even close to what the first person whispered. Over the course of that short time the original whispered words have grown distorted and much more has been added to it.

So, too, a grudge. The longer you hold on to it and relive it in your mind, the more distorted it can get. The distortion of the event and not the event itself was more likely what was getting Bill so upset.

There is significant value in going back in your mind to the original incident and spending time thinking about what actually happened and what factors came into play. Often you will find that many grudges you've been holding against your partner have more to do with your own unrealistic expectations than with the actual offense your partner committed. It is those expectations that are really causing most of the trouble. Like Bill, you have expanded those charges in your mind and now each time you bring up a grudge it has so much more behind it because of what you have let it become. No wonder your grudges against your partner make you feel miserable, angry and unloving toward them.

In order to stop holding onto grudges you have to accept that many of them are molehills that grew into mountains. Those mountains have been built on small hurts or disappointments that you didn't deal with when they happened as well as holding onto unrealistic expectations of your partner. To coin a phrase, you can't always get what you want. But who proclaims you are entitled to get everything you want? You need to balance the positives you do get from the relationship with the disappointments that come when you don't get what you want, what you think you should get, what you feel you deserve.

You need to reflect on what initially caused you to hold a particular grudge without coloring it with all it could or might mean. Rate the actual incident in your mind. Does that rating really warrant what you have let it become? Looking again at the example of Bill and Paula, once he finally was able to examine her actual offense of forgetting his birthday that one time, he admitted he put much more significance on it than it deserved. As he talked about other grudges he held against Paula, he saw that many of them were generated more from a naive view of what he wanted rather than a realistic view. He was finally able to realize that the many positives in their relationship far outweighed the slights that he had been harboring as grudges.

In looking at your own relationship we strongly suggest that you sort out what grudges are misdemeanors and which are felonies. If your partner has been unfaithful, abuses alcohol or drugs, has been intentionally cruel—these are serious infractions. If you harbor them as grudges instead of dealing with them swiftly and fully, these grudges are relationship killers and personal emotional destroyers. Even if your partner makes positive changes—stops having affairs, gets help with abuse problems, stops being cruel—it may not be enough for you.

Let's use the example of Grace and Jerry. They've been together for nearly fifteen years. Five years ago Jerry had an affair with a colleague. It didn't last long and he confessed his infidelity soon afterward. Grace was devastated and felt she could never trust Jerry again. She held this act as an understandably serious grudge against him. But they had two children and Jerry vowed it would never happen again, so Grace agreed to stay in the marriage. And after that Jerry did try to reassure her by being as transparent as possible about everything he was doing. He also began devoting more time to Grace and his children and made every effort to win back her trust. Still, Grace could not let it go. They came into couples counseling with me about a year ago. Grace admitted that Jerry was trying his best but she just couldn't let the grudge go even when she saw that it was killing her relationship with Jerry. They had come to a crossroads. Either she could work hard to finally let the grudge go or she had to end the relationship. This is a process we are still working on.

You should be clear by now that whatever caused the grudges you have, whether a misdemeanor or felony, grudges never do you any good.

And although your partner may not have a clue as to how many grudges you are holding against them, they certainly are aware that you're not happy or satisfied with them. In turn, it is likely they are accumulating grudges of their own. When a couple is weighted down with grudges, the resentment is toxic and the relationship becomes an unsightly miserable mess.

To make your relationship a healthy happy place to live you must deal with the unwieldy unhealthy clutter first. But even when you reach the point of wanting to let go of grudges and clean up your act, you may not know how to actually rid your mind of them. Learning how to let go of grudges is an easy process to grasp. But, like the game of chess, it takes a long time to master. You need to do it over and over again.

Let's try this technique I learned from Dr. Fred Luskin, Director of the Stanford University Forgiveness Projects. First close your eyes and think about a specific grudge. Picture it in your mind. Go over it in as much detail as you can. When did it happen? Picture the time of day, time of year. Who else besides your partner was present? Picture them. Create the scene as fully and accurately as you can. Now picture the event itself. Who said what? Who did what? Relive it. Hold it there and notice your breathing and the amount of tension in your body. Notice how you are feeling emotionally and physically.

Reliving the grudge likely increases your breathing and heightens your tension.

Now clear the vision from your mind and take a few slow deep breaths. Relax your body. Let go of any tension you are feeling. Once you are more relaxed there are three options: one is doing what Bill did, allowing himself to review the actual incident and consider the realities of what was going on for Paula and evaluate the reality of his own expectations. A second option is called rewriting the grudge. Change the story. Rescript it. Picture a more successful outcome. Another option is simply to close your eyes and picture a pleasant scene, one that makes you feel happy. It can be a real scene or an imaginary one. It could be sitting with your child on your lap reading a story; it could be a fantasy island with warm tropical winds. Let your imagination go free. Notice how you're feeling now. Relaxed. Content. Happy. Stress is gone.

Now open your eyes and try to hold onto that happy feeling for a while.

Pick the one(s) that works best for you. Once you can systematically use your chosen technique every time a grudge pops into your head, you will slowly but surely prevent that grudge from continuing to lodge itself in your brain.

Knowing that the grudges themselves make you stressed and the work involved in ridding yourself of grudges can also be stressful, keep in mind that there are additional ways to alleviate stress such as learning relaxation techniques, meditation, yoga, and other mind-body approaches. The point is the less stress you feel the more available you are to continue to clean up the mess.

When you are able to toss out your grudges you will not only be getting rid of the mess you will reap many other benefits. You will feel empowered. You will feel good to be taking charge of your life, taking responsibility for it. The more grudges you toss the lighter your load. You will feel better physically as well. You will feel less stress, less muscle tension, more relaxed. When you let go of grudges you will feel freer to give and receive more love from your partner. In short, you become more open to creating a positive, healthy relationship.

One way of looking at it is that when you chose to let go of grudges you chose to lighten your own negative spiritual burden. You give yourself permission to lighten your own load of ugly, unloving feelings. Instead of obsessing about each and every wrong that has been done you, you chose to let your rancid feelings go, to stop torturing yourself with harbored anger. Whether or not you can forgive your partner for any specific word or deed, by letting a grudge go you will feel better and freer. Once the pressure has lifted you will have a clearer mind as to how you want to handle the originating event that made you turn it into a grudge. We want to emphasize that forgiving doesn't mean forgetting. Just as important, remembering doesn't mean persevering. If you handle a grudge as if it is a molehill it will not grow into a mountain.

We understand that you cannot always toss out a grudge. But you can reshape it or come to terms with some negative feelings by making peace with them. A friend's therapist put it very effectively: You have chosen a particular person to partner up with—learn to love them for who they actually are rather than spending a lifetime disappointed that they are not some cherished fantasy creature. There has to be a certain degree of acceptance of the person you love being who they are. Making peace with some of your negative feelings will keep them from holding so much significance in your mind and go a long way towards building more acceptance.

Part Two
Best Practices

Guidelines that are used to obtain the most efficient and effective way of completing a task using repeatable and proven procedures.

Chapter Five
Begin with the Basics

The bedrock skills of Relationship Cleanup will set you on the right course in your relationship and provide solutions to keep it running smoothly. The concepts and skills you will acquire here are simple in nature, mostly intuitive, and deeply practical. The trick is to employ them early and often to keep your emotional clutter at bay.

We understand that it's hard to change patterns and habits. It takes commitment and effort even when your current habits are doing neither you nor your partner any good. So many bad habits, so much emotional debris. Typically, neat home gurus favor tackling the mountain of mess in little chunks—starting with one drawer and a small one at that. The same holds true for relationship cleanups. Start with a small change. The smaller the better. As your skills and confidence increase, move on up.

We'll help you get started with a few fast and easy suggestions. By following these tips you will see immediate improvement in your relationship. These suggestions derive from our own clinical and personal experiences. We expect they'll look quite familiar and obvious to you. You were surely doing most of this by instinct when you first fell in love. These basic "do's" come naturally when you're in a romantic thrall. Sadly, over time it is just as "natural" to lose that romantic frame of mind. How many of these good behaviors have been relegated to your relational storage bin? Let this be your wake-up call. Dig these romantic notions back out and once more make them second nature to you.

Have a positive mindset. Try thinking of these suggestions as ways to woo your partner all over again. At the very least you'll feel lighter and refreshed, reminding your partner of better times past and better times to come. If you are lucky your partner will be inspired by your leadership and try to get in on the action.

Begin your relationship cleanup here. These positive steps make your relationship easier to maintain by creating fewer places for dirt to accumulate. Follow any one of these 5 tips—whichever seems easiest—and your life together will be a little bit less of a mess.

Say yes
Say I'm sorry
Say I'm empathic
Say I'm on board
Say I love you

The virtues of our DO LIST are likely to bristle some feathers. Buried in the morass of a long term relationship these old saws don't sound so easy or smart any more. The messy slog of an ongoing relationship can make us almost cynical about romantic love. Questions, no doubt, are popping into your minds.

—Say yes to what? What am I supposed to be sorry about? Obviously I'm on my partner's side. Doesn't that go without saying? Say I'm on board? On board with what? I'm not going on some hair-brained trip just because my partner wants to go somewhere I have no desire to go? And—glaringly—I wouldn't be with my partner without loving them. Shouldn't that go without saying?

For some disenchanted individuals and couples the value of these seemingly obvious virtues takes some explaining. Here's what we suggest you make happen and why.

Say yes.

Seek out opportunities to say "yes" to your partner when they ask something of you. Yes is a statement of inclusion. With a "yes," you affirm that the connection you share with your partner is important to you. Their pleasure is something you value. Yes will brighten not only your partner's spirit but yours as well. Every yes is a gift.

Recently a client told me with some pride that he tried out the "yes" strategy when his wife asked him to bring in the empty trashcan from the driveway to the garage. She looked surprised when he readily agreed. Applying our tip he immediately carried out the task—no delay tactics, no complaints like why couldn't one of their kids do it. Back from his little chore, he was the one who was more than a bit surprised, not to mention pleased, to see the big smile of pleasure on his wife's face. It set the whole evening on a better, happier note. Of course the novelty of his gesture amped up its impact, but a shared life nurtured with these little "gifts" has got to feel warmer.

Now think for a minute how often you say "no" to your partner, both directly and indirectly. Your partner asks, "Would you make me a cup of coffee? Could you run to the store for me? Can you do me a favor? Would you please take care ..." You say "No," possibly followed by a list of excuses. You're too tired, too busy, maybe annoyed about something your partner did earlier and so you don't want to be accommodating. Or you simply see no reason why your partner can't just do it.

A verbal "no" isn't necessary to show disengagement. You only have to cast a certain look, find yourself distracted and not really listening, groan or roll your eyes. You get the idea. When you say "no" however you express it, it is a statement of rejection. It can maintain distance. No can be dirty laundry spilling over. It's unsightly. Too many "no's" is unhygienic. It's not a happy way to live together.

Elise and I were fortunate to realize early on in our relationship that saying yes to each other gave us both so much more pleasure than saying no. Whenever possible we try to meet the each other's wants and needs within reason. And a request that is within reason is an important barometer. It's not always simple or easy to honestly discern whether a request your partner makes is reasonable. I remember one occasion some time ago when I didn't give a particular request by Elise enough careful thought. For that matter, neither did she.

Our son was an infant at the time. Elise was home caring for him but this one morning she woke up with bad stomach upset. She felt so sick she asked me if I could take David with me to work. It was a Saturday and I only had one patient but I really didn't think it was a good idea. But she felt awful and so I said yes.

The results were as poor as one might imagine and then some. Mid session I had to stop and change our infant. My new patient left in horror, and, understandably, never returned. What was I thinking? Clearly, not enough. In hindsight, both Elise and I realized she had made an unreasonable request and I should have said no and, more importantly, we should have put our heads together to come up with other more practical solutions.

Fortunately most yeses are simply not that risky to support. Even if Elise asks for something she could do herself or vice versa we tend to say yes to each other because it simply feels good to be nice and it creates a warm, positive, loving environment for both of us.

Elise asks me to fill her weekly pill case for her, which is something she could do for herself very easily. But it really takes so little out of me. It relieves her of some mysterious pillbox stress she suffers from and adds to my husbandly value. Fifty years ago we might have spent hours discussing her expressed need. These days her request seems an opportunity for me to make her life a tiny bit better. Long discussion, short discussion, no discussion—whatever the path—we each gain from my "yes".

Of course it works both ways. I asked Elise to take care of the household bills. Now, the truth is, neither one of us likes that job. So it becomes a question of who minds it the most. Elise and I were both able to agree that I minded it more. So she said "yes" and took over the task. Relieved of my juvenile distaste of accounting my stress level diminished and I felt happier and grateful. That made her happier—though not about doing the bills.

These two examples demonstrate how unequal the giving may be from time to time. It is way more demanding to pay the bills that to fill the pillbox. We don't keep score and you shouldn't either. Give as much as you can, as wholeheartedly as you can and your love relationship will be the winner.

Yes says you're committed to promoting your relationship health. Yes creates an environment full of support, cooperation and affirmation. Yes protects the surfaces of your relationship from attracting crud. Yes says you want to make your partner happy. Yes has transformative powers. Try it. You'll see.

Say "I'm sorry."

Skip the explanations. Leave out the excuses. Go right to "I'm sorry" as often as you can. Then determine what you can do not to repeat the hurt and tell your partner what you will be trying not to do/say in the future.

Sometimes, during a couples consultation, I'll suggest a quick apology and hear instead, a quick "I'm not going to say 'I'm sorry' when I'm not sorry." Okay, maybe you're totally justified in what you've said or done but surely you can still open your heart and acknowledge your partner's pain. You'll both feel less isolated, which will create a better foundation for exploring the incident.

Say, a shirt you are wearing gets stained at dinner one night. If you put some stain remover on it right away there's a good chance the stain will come out in the wash and you'll be able to wear that shirt again. So too, the quicker you respond supportively to your partner's emotional pain the more productively you will be able to explore the underlying angry conflict. Most often relational anger comes from a perceived hurt or threat, or perceived indifference or disloyalty. You won't really know until you hear your partner's explanation for the hurt or anger. Were you out of line? Misunderstood? This will allow you the opportunity to re-think what you did/said and how you did/said it, rather than leaving the mess lying around for some other time. A time you may never actually get to.

Crucially, saying I'm sorry should be your way of opening the problem for discussion—not as a way to shut your partner up.

Dan gets home at eight. His husband, Ed, is upset:

Ed (angrily): You are so inconsiderate. Couldn't you at least have the courtesy to text me if you know you'll be late?

Dan (defensively): I'm not so late. I come home at eight plenty of nights.

Ed – But we talked about going to the movies tonight and now it's too late. Obviously you don't think what I want matters...

This kind of argument can go on and on, becoming ever messier and uglier. But let's stop it here. Let's imagine instead that Dan simply responded, "I'm sorry I got you so upset." Then harkening back to DO #1 said, "I promise I'll text you when I have a change of plans that affects us." In this second go-round Ed's non-defensive stance lets his husband know that he cares and wants to resolve the problem with him. The big payoff here is moving from opposition and pain to cooperation and trust—reinforcing the relational rewards of being on the same side.

Say "I care."

When Geena and Mike were dating they showed each other they cared in so many ways. Listening attentively to each other, being sympathetic, doing little special things—Mike gave Geena a book he thought she would like. Geena made Mike his favorite chocolate pudding when he was under the weather. They cared about each other and it was easy to demonstrate it. Each was thrilled to be with someone who showed that they cared. They really tried to "get" each other. They took endless interest in what each other's lives were like and how each felt about everything.

With hardly any history as a couple, Geena and Mike's focus was on getting to know each other, primarily to learn about their lives before they met. A few years together and, caught up in the press of everyday life, they've lost their enthusiasm for making the effort to understand each other:

Mike: We really need to talk about what happened this morning. Your daughter promised she wouldn't be on her phone during breakfast and you just sat there and let her get away with it. Again."

Geena (sighing): "Our daughter. And can we please talk about it later, I'm on my way to the gym."

Another example:

Geena comes home from work very upset about something her boss did and shares her upset with Mike.

Mike: (looks up from his computer, gives Geena an impatient scowl and turns back to the screen) How many times have I told you you have to stop letting him get away with that crap. You never listen!

Really? Who is not listening here? His wife wants to let off steam in a safe place and instead she ends up feeling frustrated, dismissed, uncared for. To give Mike the benefit of the doubt, maybe he felt impatient with Geena, as they'd hashed this issue through enough times. His show of exasperation, unfortunately, is not only unhelpful to their relationship, it cuts off the opportunity for communication and the chance for emotional intimacy. When they were falling in love Mike looked for any opportunity to demonstrate how much he cared. These days he's lost the knack or has forgotten how necessary it is to demonstrate the caring he feels inside.

As a relationship grows, we'll sometimes feel short-changed by our partners and we'll short-change them as well. Fact of life. But when impatience and lack of curiosity become routine, feelings of anger and frustration mount. Arguments get more intense, differences of opinion and style more threatening. Freshen up your relationship by going back to showing how much you care.

Paying attention conveys caring; striving to understand what your partner wants shows caring; curbing your irritation is a caring gesture. Your partnership once thrived on the perception of caring. The longer you are together the greater the value of getting back to basics. To be perfectly trite: there is no time like the present to start your refresh.

It's not that you have to become some sort of full-time all caring saint. Only an actual saint could do that. Us regular folks can only aspire to do better. Elise and I slip up, make mistakes, take wrong turns often enough. It's easy to get distracted, overwhelmed by other issues, get just too busy. We all face myriad challenges inside and outside of our relationships that distract us from working hard to be happy together.

Fight the buildup of muck. Whenever possible, DO take the time to be interested and concerned. Missed opportunities to show empathy leave both of you feeling something is lost that you once shared. But it isn't necessarily lost for all time, it's merely hidden under the day to day grime.

Let's take another example. I've been treating Jim and his partner Diane for several months. Diane has a lot of problems with her aging mother. This has been an issue since their courtship. Back then Jim would go with Diane to visit her mother in her home. If she had errands to do for her mother, Jim pitched in. He was there for her and comforted her whenever he could. Now they've been married several years and Diane's mother is being moved to a nursing home. Diane feels burdened and overwhelmed by the challenges in caring for her. Jim has tended to leave this problem on his wife's plate. He has plenty of problems of his own and this has been going on for a long time. It's understandable that Jim would feel like he is running out of steam here, but if you think about it, what would it really take out of Jim to express compassion and understanding for what Diane is going through? What I helped him to realize was that it would benefit them both.

Showing compassion brings you and your partner closer together. You are bridging the alienation gap by demonstrating interest in each other's feelings about whatever you're each experiencing. It's showing your partner respect and not being judgmental. This is something you already know how to do and have just forgotten to continue doing it. When you go out of your way to show your partner compassion and responsiveness you are taking another important step in creating a healthy, happy relationship.

Say "I'm on board."

When your partner asks you to join them in an activity that you're less than keen on doing, instead of a million questions about why the trip, the party, the shopping jaunt is necessary or desired, try the power of "I'll join you since you really want me there with you." Yes, this is another chance to say "yes." And no, you don't have to be on board every time your partner suggests something to do, but take into account how often you have not been a good sport. Before you opt out consider the opportunity for creating goodwill and camaraderie with your partner. Think of how being on board will benefit both of you.

Again, let's go back to when you were dating, when you first fell in love. We suspect you couldn't get enough of each other. You'd go places and do things with each other just to be together. It didn't matter if you were all that interested or thrilled with the actual event. You were thrilled with being on board. You loved pleasing your date, they loved pleasing you. That was the right idea. It still is.

What if you are the type who feels manipulated when your partner makes a claim on your time? Maybe your mom seemed to be manipulated by your dad and you vowed that wouldn't happen to you. In your gut you're vigilant for any hint of outside control. And, perhaps, this blinds you to the difference between control and cooperation—the difference between being made to clean up your room and choosing to because it's family clean up time. Try rethinking a request for participation as a welcome opportunity to make your partner feel valued.

There is a crucial difference between choosing an advantageous course of action and merely giving in to social pressure. If you are feeling manipulated or controlled you are not a willing participant. You are going along because you feel you have no choice. You believe you will pay for it if you don't go along. And if you feel controlled your actions and behavior will show it and result in both of you collecting antipathy. Going along when you are sporting a bad attitude is likely to backfire. Review the advantages of joining in, replace your defensive avoidance with a willing desire to participate or your good intentions will backfire.

When Elise and I were first dating she asked me to go with her to a family picnic. It was the last thing my teenage self wanted to do. Meet the whole family? Make small talk with them? Be charming to old people? Well, you all can relate, I'm sure. I voiced my objections. Elise heard me out and sympathized—which helped. It turned out she didn't feel very differently than I about family gatherings, but thought having her boyfriend with her would make it easier for her. I felt flattered and chose to go with her. Once I felt willing I stopped feeling manipulated. Since then the please join me issue has surfaced in countless situations. Working relationships are enhanced by each of you being good sports. DO choose to join your partner because it's the caring thing to do then take the opportunity to relearn the joy of shared experience.

Whenever you take the opportunity to join in enthusiastically you and your partner will feel closer because you're showing your loved one that you enjoy being with them even if you're not all that keen on the actual event. This is a statement of love. You act loving, your partner feels loved and that love provides a very successful cleansing for both of you.

It's no different than pitching in to get your home cleaned up. If you participate willingly you are showing your partner that you care and want to help. Your partner feels good, in turn you feel good, and you discover that you can have a good time together even when engaged in a mundane housekeeping activity.

Which brings us to – say "I love you."

You can say it verbally and simply – I love you. You can say it in little actions. Wash the dishes on occasion, remember to take out the trash, give your partner a compliment. What's important is to feel the love behind these words and deeds and not just the habit.

Not to say the habit is a bad one. Elise and I have the habit of saying I love you when either of us leaves for work or just before we hang up the phone after even a brief conversation with each other or before we go to sleep. What makes these habitual expressions more than habit is about what these words mean to us. Saying I love you is actually less habit and more ritual. A loving ritual.

Remember how easily, how joyously it once was to say, "I love you." Your love bubbled up inside of you and overflowed. Those loving feelings extended to observing your partner's wonderful qualities or actions and complimenting them. When you're in that romantic haze, saying, "I love you" literally fell off your tongue. It's time to get in touch again with your loving feelings for your partner. Share those feelings. The words "I love you" never get old.

When you survey the landscape of your relationship it is likely scattered with all kinds of emotional debris. Simple acts of love, support, kindness, participation, and companionship will go a long way in cleaning up the detritus and it will have a strong positive impact on your relationship. You and your partner will both feel lighter, brighter, happier and healthier the more often you make the time and effort to follow our tips.

Chapter Six
Get The Wax Out

If you let wax build up on your furniture the gloss will be gone. If you let the wax build up in your ears, the shine will fade from your relationship. Listening is the crucial step to having a clean, bright relationship. Sharpen up your listening skills. Get ready to listen. Being distracted, too busy, indifferent, or stressed all cause wax build-up and block your ability to listen.

How often have you either said or heard these words – Are you listening? Unfortunately, we often aren't really listening. Listening is different from merely hearing words being spoken. When your partner asks you if you're listening or if you ask it of them, what is really meant is—Are you paying attention? Are you connecting with what I'm saying? Do you understand what I'm trying to get across to you?

The more you practice your listening skills, the better. Make it your daily homework. Focus when your partner is speaking to you. Give them your full attention. Hopefully most of what you listen to will be mundane everyday communication. Listen to your partner with the goal of really knowing their current thoughts and feelings. We've called this practice Conversation for the Purpose of Understanding. When you listen to each other you enhance the perception that you are loved for who you actually are and not as an unrealistic fantasy. When you can listen and then share your feelings you and your partner will gain more insight into each other. Getting into the mind and heart of your partner as they develop and change over time will create true closeness in place of fading romantic illusions.

Listening in general is a good practice. In the best of times it will certainly be an easier task than when there are problems. But in all relationships problems inevitably arise. Problems can be within your relationship or your partner may bring up a problem or issue that they are dealing with outside the relationship. It could be a problem with a friend, a colleague, a parent, whomever. When your partner wants to talk something over, choose to be thankful to be included in their world. There are many times when you and your partner are both comfortable and capable of dealing with outside problems on your own. But when your partner expresses the need or desire to share any of these issues or problems with you, this becomes another prime time to pay attention and listen.

Clear your mind of other distractions. Put away your smartphone! Give them the attention they deserve, the attention you'd desire in a similar instance. Listen. What does your partner need from you? Do they merely want your empathy, your understanding, your support, or do they want actual suggestions or advice as to how they might solve a particular dilemma?

If you don't know what is wanted of you, ask. Too often, when your partner presents a problem your first inclination might be to jump right in and try to help them regardless of their needs. I have had a number of clients over the years that tell me that their partners are tossing out solutions practically before they've even gotten through explaining the problem. I have the tendency to do this at times with Elise. My motivation is two-fold—I want to make her feel better and I want to get the problem solved quickly so it doesn't interfere with our good times. Can you see that I've twisted the communication around to be about my needs and interests? Elise doesn't end up feeling better; merely frustrated with me at best.

If your partner wants nothing more from you than to listen and sympathize or act as their sounding board try to give them exactly that. If they do seem to want your help or advice, it is still best to clarify their wishes.

Let's say your partner asks for your help cleaning up the basement. You graciously say yes. Great. You got that "yes" tip down. But wait. You can still run into trouble. If, instead of pitching in to help with what your partner needs help doing, you begin questioning everything they want to keep or toss; or you keep telling them how they should attack the clutter and/or explain the way you would do it, did you really listen to them? Are you really helping your partner? If anything, you are likely making the task harder, in the process engendering their frustration, even rage.

Listening to your partner in these instances means giving them the attention they deserve, expressing empathy and understanding, encouraging them to tell you what they need from you and helping them by doing what they need.

The time to really make certain the wax is fully out of your ears is when your partner expresses a serious problem or crisis within your relationship. Your partner may begin with—"Can we talk?" or "Is this a good time to discuss something with you?" Your heart sinks. You feel a twinge of dread. This means trouble. You just know your partner wants to bring up something that's bothering them, likely something for which you are going to be blamed.

It's hard to listen when your partner is upset, especially when it's about something you've said or done. No one enjoys being on the receiving end of hurt, disappointed, angry feelings. You are likely to experience a fight/flight response when this happens. Attack your attacker or flee to safety. Your powerful, primitive instinct is to protect yourself at all costs, leaving your relationship to take the hit in your place. Failing to hear your partner out in a timely fashion, because you've taken an offensive or a defensive stance, makes a mess of your partner's effort to clean up the mess they perceive. And your relationship tidying efforts will fall by the wayside.

I can almost always tell when Elise is about to bring up an issue she's unhappy about that involves me. I see it in her serious expression, her whole tense body language. Many of us have the ability to read our loved ones before so much as one word is spoken. We know a bomb's about to drop and all we can think about is we don't want to be the target.

If your partner has a complaint about what's happening in your relationship you need to hear it so you can work together to address the mess. Take a breath, relax your body if you can, and focus on listening.

This is the time when high quality listening is the most important. Never blow these moments off.

Let's say it really isn't a good time to hear your partner out. You've got to be somewhere soon or people are coming over, or you have something you must do, or you're too distracted and don't feel you can deal with any more issues right at that moment. You need to present your partner with an appointment time (not too long in the future) when you will give them your full attention. You are creating a sacred relational contract to bring wax free ears to the impending discussion.

When the time comes, sit down and face your loved one. Concentrate on what's being said and not on planning how you are going to defend yourself or retaliate. Most important, avoid getting locked in a vicious cycle of charges and counter-charges. That's like tossing your garbage back and forth. The garbage ends up spilling all over the place, smelling bad and you both end up disgusted.

Let's say you are listening hard to your upset partner but aren't sure you get the point. Don't jump to conclusions. Don't try to show how clever you are by telling them what they really mean and how wrong they are. Keep quiet. Continue to listen. Wait and see if your partner has even more to say now that they have your attention and they're not feeling disregarded or overpowered by you. Make eye contact, nod encouragingly. Your caring, supportive expression will shore up your partner's confidence in the process of relationship maintenance. Your effort to be present, despite your stress, will make the moment better for your partner.

Once your partner appears to you to have said their piece, you can make sure by gently prodding them. Can you tell me more about it? Is there any more you want to say about the problem?

When your partner has truly done saying all they have to say, it is helpful to repeat or at least paraphrase what you believe they are saying, ie: what you are hearing. This playback will help both you and your partner see if you've got it right. If you have, your partner will be greatly relieved to have been correctly heard. If you haven't gotten it right, it gives them the chance to clarify what they're trying to communicate.

Now it's your turn to speak. But before you do, remember to maintain the proper mind-set. Even if you feel your partner is being unfairly accusatory or judgmental in their approach, leaving you feeling angry, hurt, misunderstood, we encourage you to take an extra moment. Breathe. Give yourself a chance to think.

Right here and now, ask yourself whether there is any truth to your partner's issue with you. Try not to be thin-skinned. Accept that you are capable of making mistakes. And if you realize you shouldn't have said or done something, or could have handled a situation better, here's a great time to simply say and mean "I'm sorry." If you really think you are being maligned you might still have reason to say, "I'm sorry." But now you're saying you're feeling concern for your partner—sorry for your partner's pain. You have become a relational hero.

Should you be exhausted, stressed out, hoarding complaints of your own, this is potentially a time when garbage can again get thrown around and that's only going to make the situation worse. Before you allow yourself to reply harshly, remember, as Terrence Real strongly advises, that the person you are addressing has been your beloved partner—not your enemy. Instead of flinging dirt, express your feelings without going on the attack.

Mastering the pattern of sharing concerns and resolving them equitably is key to preventing the accumulation of emotional distress. This is not an easy task. You can easily find yourself slipping into a self-preservation mode. This can spark anger, resentment, and indignation. The temptation to strike back can at times be powerful.

Always keep in mind who it is you are listening to—your first love, your soul mate, your intimate partner, the mother/father of your children. This is the person you have chosen to share your life with. They are telling you there is a problem between you that is bothering them. How do you think you should respond if you honestly want to resolve the problem?

An approach I've taken with my couples when one partner is expressing a concern and the other partner jumps into attack mode is what I call the boss test: I address the attacker—"Is your stance or your words anything you'd express to your boss." Individuals who would never risk an angry confrontation with their employer for fear of risking their job might think nothing of telling their partner off, yelling at them, threatening one thing or another...saying all the terrible things they'd never say to a boss, a co-worker or even one of their employees because they know it's inappropriate or they're afraid of retaliation. Yet they're oblivious to the mess that develops when they are verbally abusive to the person nearest and dearest to them.

Occasionally, working with very indignant individuals, I resort to a crude but sometimes effective strategy. "Will that response get you laid?" I ask. I want to shock them into the realization that putting their partner on the defensive is unlikely to get them more affection.

Think about how your words will affect your partner. Is your intent really to be hurtful to this person you love? No matter what the issue, no matter how hurt, angry, or frustrated you are feeling, your best interest is not in hurting them back, and not in closing the door and shutting your partner out. Hold on. Listen hard. Then speak with moderation, remembering that your goal is not to derail the process but to successfully accomplish a mutual goal.

Sometimes the goal may be to agree to disagree about a particular issue. You both have your points, your explanations, and you each own your own feelings. In this situation the positive outcome may simply be showing respect and acceptance for each other's differences. Remember, that's a far better result than letting a battle turn into a war.

An incident happened in my office while we were working on this book that highlighted the value of listening actively verses listening as passive engagement. I was teaching Marian and Robert about the value of quiet, active listening when Marian spoke up, "Oh he'll listen to me for hours when I'm upset about something he's done but when I've said my piece he literally clams up. Doesn't even say, 'I'm sorry.'"

If listening only leaves you silent, you aren't helping much. Lacking any response your partner is left high and dry. Did you understand the problem? Did you hear anything at all? You might think you are being a perfect listener when, in effect, you are merely dishing out the silent treatment. Your partner has just risked opening up only to be left holding the garbage bag. On the other hand, when you listen and then respond in a mindful, considerate way you are giving your partner the gift of understanding. Show some real understanding and you've replaced the world of feeling dismissed, attacked, demeaned, with the possibility of reviving the romantic elation of first finding the one who truly understood you.

Your bond will grow stronger and healthier as you each feel comforted hearing each other out in good times and bad. Put your listening skills to work resolving conflicts or exploring life struggles. Quality listening endows your relationship with a protective shine. The more you each can rely on feeling heard, the easier it will be to clean up each relational mess as it arises.

Don't listen like you care. Listen because you care!

Chapter Seven
Have A Clean Up Plan

If you want a clean house you will do a better job if you follow certain rules or guidelines. You'll start with the right attitude even if only to accept that you need to tidy up. (Parents are coming, you're having a dinner party, or the place is such a mess even you can't stand it any more.) You'll think about what you must do—dust, vacuum, wash down the floors, scrub the toilet etc. If you use the right tools and know how to use them, the work will be easier and more effective. If you and your partner are going to do this together, figure out who's going to do what and when. Create a timeline and stick to it. Not only will a cleaner home be the outcome, so too will a good feeling of cooperation and achievement.

Like the rules for cleaning up your home effectively there are useful guideposts for cleaning up a messy dysfunctional relationship. Both promote the need for a positive attitude, cooperation, and mastery of a few special techniques. Like our earlier tips, we encourage you to consider each of these guidelines seriously and try to apply them to your relationship for maximum benefit. They are all designed to help you and your loved one do things right in the first place, creating the most mess free environment in which love has the best chance to survive.

Treat your loved one as you want them to treat you.
Make your loved one your first priority.
Be kind and caring to your loved one.

Be open to compromise.

A cleanup is successful when both of you feel like winners.

Arguing is fine but never pull out the rug.

Wipe up the mildew before it turns to toxic mold.

Express gratitude.

Focus on the good rather than the bad.

Treasure each improvement.

Treat your loved one as you want them to treat you.

You're right if you are thinking – that's basically the Golden Rule (Do unto others as you would have others do unto you.) Exactly! But also think about how often that rule is forgotten. When someone is being thoughtless, dismissive, abusive to their loved one, it's hard to imagine they would want their loved one to treat them the same way. But it happens all the time between couples that are in very unhygienic relationships.

Your partner is accusing you of creating a relational mess. You can't imagine what all the fuss is about. What have you done or said that was so upsetting? In general, although we are finely tuned to taking offence when others, especially our loved ones, hurt or anger us, we are not so clear about the harm we might inadvertently cause them by our words or actions.

Your partner is hurt or angry and calls you on it. There are several possible reactions. You may agree that you were a little thoughtless or callous, so you apologize and try to do better. You may cop to the accusation but think your partner is overreacting. You may disagree with the accusation and dismiss your partner's complaint. You don't get what they are so upset about. It's easy enough to apply the Golden Rule when you and your partner are on the same wavelength. It starts to get messy when you don't get where they are coming from or why. You wouldn't be upset if your partner said or did the same thing to you so why is your partner getting so carried away?

You think you're following the Golden Rule, but there's a deeper layer to that rule when it comes to intimate relationships. It's not simply do unto your partner as you would have them do unto you. First you need to understand what they think you did—see your words or actions from their point of view. Just because something wouldn't hurt or offend you doesn't mean it wouldn't hurt or offend your partner. Here the Golden Rule requires you and your partner to be aware and sympathetic to each other's feelings and sensitivities. Knock yourself out trying not to hurt your partner and hold your partner to the same standard.

The Golden Rule also comes into play when you are far more caring and thoughtful towards others than towards your partner. Here's a typical example:

Kathy comes into my office and she is fit to be tied. Her husband, Brad is a town manager and she complains that not a day passes that someone doesn't come up to her to extol her husband's virtues. He's so caring, so helpful, so kind. He goes out of his way for everyone. Everyone, Kathy tells me between clenched teeth, except her. At home he's distracted, inattentive, unhelpful, and Kathy feels that he takes her for granted. It has become more than a sore spot for Kathy. She is angry, disillusioned, frustrated. It colors their whole relationship. Brad definitely needs to clean up his act at home if he and Kathy are going to make their relationship work.

Elise and I have heard this particular theme all too often in working with couples. Barbara bemoans to Elise: The face Jack shows in public is not the one he shows when we're alone. He saves his charm, generosity and kindness for everyone else. With me, he's complaining about money or he's lost in whatever he's doing on his cell phone or griping about having to go out to dinner with friends. But when we are at the restaurant, he's warm and engaging. Occasionally he'll even pick up the tab. And I'm staring at my husband thinking why can't he be this way with me?

A valid question. Okay, sometimes it's easier to be thoughtful, generous, kind to people with whom you don't have an intimate relationship. You don't spend that much time with them, you don't have a history together, so you feel you can afford to go that extra mile. You may go to someone's home for dinner and you help the host clear up the table, maybe even help load the dishwasher. What a guy! The guests think you're great. So attentive, so helpful. Meanwhile your partner is steaming. If they only knew!

Clean up your mess where it really counts. Apply the kindnesses and thoughtfulness with which your treat others to your loved one. Although it takes more effort more often, the rewards are greater. The Golden Rule works well in general, but it works to great effect when you apply it to your loved one. Treat others well, treat your loved one best. Just as you want to be treated best by the one you love.

Make your loved one your first priority.

Life holds so many obligations, responsibilities, and social activities. Look at your calendar. Is it filled with appointments, engagements? How often do you have to juggle priorities, make decisions about what to do, when to do it, who you will have to disappoint, who you feel you need to please?

Juggle as much as you must, but don't pick your partner to be the one to disappoint. The more often they aren't your top priority, the more your relationship suffers. The more often they are your top priority, the more often you will be theirs.

When you can't put your loved one first at a particular time, let them know why. Ask for their understanding. Let them see that they are still first on your thoughts. That sentiment will be appreciated. Your partner will be grateful to know how much they are valued even if there are times it's not possible to put them first. They see that they are first on your mind, first in your heart. That is a great feeling—great for them and great for you. Where there might have been tension and stress (and you would both feel it in your own way) there is now harmony. Precisely what you both want. And, really, it just takes a little effort. It's a matter of being mindful. Mindfulness will save you and your partner from the dirty clutter that grows from thoughtless words and deeds.

Be kind and caring to your loved one and let them be kind and caring to you.

Being kind and caring to your loved one is as important as being kind and caring to yourself and to your personal space. This requires attentiveness and understanding. Understanding is key here. Do you really know how your partner wants you to show them kindness, caring?

Does your partner know how to show you kindness, caring? Are they negligent when it comes to showing these feelings? Do they try and fail? Do either of you really get the rewards that should come from this mutual give and take?

We have a friend, Barbara, who, every time she has a cold, her husband runs out to get her chicken soup. When she tells us this, she sighs and says, "I know he's just trying to show how much he cares, but…" She never asked for chicken soup. She doesn't like chicken soup. She would have been happy with a cup of tea. She would have been happy if he simply closed the door and let her sleep. Elise asks if she ever told him this. Again she sighs. "Of course, but he just thinks I don't want to put him out. He insists on showing me that he'll drive to the ends of the earth for me."

Being kind and caring to your partner and having those feelings reciprocated is often easier than you might think it is. If Barbara's husband had not only listened to her but believed what she was saying, and simply got her tea and closed the door so she could rest, he would have shown true kindness, caring and most important, true understanding. The soup – well, the soup wasn't appreciated at all. Now, if the tables were reversed, very likely he would have loved having her bring him that chicken soup. But it wasn't about him. Now, I do wonder, if her husband was sick would she bring him chicken soup. Or would she bring him the tea she would have wanted?

Be open to compromise.

Couples often equate compromise with capitulation. Compromise is not the same as buckling under. Compromise means coming to a mutually acceptable agreement in order to chose a course of action that seems promising to both of you. Your relationship will feel rejuvenated and empowered when your compromise creates an exciting fresh course of action.

When you disagree about what to do, acknowledge together the opportunity to be a winning team. It can feel great to clarify your competing views and chose a happy balance. It can feel even better when the result is a new idea you both love.

Keep in mind the familiar adage – Give a little, get a little

On Elise's last birthday I wanted to throw her a big birthday bash; she told me she didn't want a large party. At first I thought she was concerned about the cost. Even when she said that wasn't it, I didn't really believe her. I considered making it a surprise party as a way to avoid further discussion, my thought being she'll be happy once she's there. I am very lucky I didn't follow through with that idea. She guessed my plan and got very angry. Well, actually we both ended up angry – Elise for my disregarding her wishes, me for not being appreciated for my generosity.

The situation is familiar enough and, no doubt, you can envision easy solutions (somehow it's often easier to solve other couples' problems) – we could have an intimate gathering and I would let Elise pick out who she would want to invite; we could have a very special and expensive date night, or a weekend in the Bahamas. The solution we ultimately worked out together was to stage a Family Getaway to Cape Cod with our kids and grandkids. It was a solution we hadn't anticipated and one that we came to by thinking outside the box. This required our willingness to let go of previously set ideas and be more creative.

Some compromises are easy to achieve. But don't be fooled. Even what seems like an easy compromise can prove challenging when neither partner is willing to give a little. Too often a standoff is created. Giving an inch feels like a mile. Individual winning or not losing takes precedence over creating a winning team.

Emotions escalate. One of you complains that you're always the one to give in, your partner complains that you're being unyielding and childish, you get angry and accuse them of always needing to have their way, they get angry at your accusation ...

Caught up in this emotional escalation you've forgotten that a successful compromise is the biggest win of all. Remember, when one of you feels like the loser, your relationship is the biggest loser of all.

A cleanup is successful when both of you feel like winners.

Have a positive attitude. Approach any mess with the goal to clean it up amicably. Before any negotiations take place, make sure you're both on the same page. Listen to each other. Be aware of your emotions and try to keep harmful ones (blame, accusation, defensiveness) in check. Don't try to outsmart or undermine your partner. Remember that in less consequential arguments it's okay to agree to disagree. When an outcome must be reached, reflect and listen as well as speak from a place of reasonableness. Whatever the outcome, treat each other with respect and kindness.

You win when the relationship wins. The relationship wins when the outcome makes you both happy to be together in life. If the compromise leaves either of you resentful it's not a good enough solution. Don't be stubborn on the one hand and don't go along to get along on the other hand. Discovering the paths that help you feel closer in the end is a challenge. But the very challenge of working together to figure out a good solution for both of you is worthwhile in and of itself. Whether both of you have to compromise on an issue or one of you needs to concede to the other to resolve a particular problem, in either case you both must strive to make the final decision one in which you feel successful. The outcome to any cleanup is never positive when the balance is tipped to the point that one of you dons the winner's apron and the other is left holding a dirty rag.

Let's look at a typical argument that might occur.

Carol "You know perfectly well I promised my sister I would go with her to a meditation program on Saturday. And you said you would watch the kids for the day. Which is something I rarely ask you to do.

Sam "I watch the kids plenty so don't give me that crap. I don't think sitting around spouting mantras is more important than my softball game. At least I'll be getting some exercise which is a hell of a lot better…"

Let's pause here. This is a perfect example of both partners starting off with the wrong attitude, a negative approach. Here, neither of them demonstrates any sign of wanting to reasonably work something out that will have the potential to be a winning resolution for both of them.

Let's replay the dispute in a positive way.

Carol - "We have a problem here. I want to go with my sister to a meditation class on Saturday and you want to play softball with your friends."

Sam - I know I said I'd watch the kids on Saturday but I totally forgot when I agreed that I had a game planned for Saturday.

Carol "Is there some way we can work this out so we can both get to do what we want?"

Sam "It would cost a pretty penny to hire a sitter for the day. And you know money is tight right now."

Carol "We could skip movie night for the next couple of weeks."

Sam "And we could barbeque hot dogs and burgers instead of steak for the picnic next Sunday."

Carol "I'll call the sitter."

Sam "And I'll take the kids to the park after school today and give you a breather."

The above example and others like it are relatively easy to work out as long as you, like Sam and Carol, focus on the specific problem, avoid accusations, irritations or disappointments, and work together cooperatively to come to a successful conclusion. In the second time round, Sam and Carol felt like their needs were being recognized and understood, and by working out a positive win-win solution, the good feelings carried over so that Sam even tossed in a bonus.

While many issues are easy to clean up successfully, some are quite difficult. A number of years back I was feeling overwhelmed and physically drained by what had grown into over fifty hours a week of work. I felt disconnected and miserable living in the suburbs. I felt the pressure of maintaining a large home and all its attendant costs. I craved some peace, wanted more time to spend with Elise and our children. We had a vacation house in the country set in the beautiful White Mountains. Whenever we were there I felt great joy and relaxation. I yearned for that on a permanent basis.

Now Elise was perfectly happy with life in the suburbs. She had friends, the kids were in a good school, they all enjoyed our home, etc. We sat up until late one night sorting through all our feelings both pro and con. It was a major issue, one that would affect all of us and so it was equally important for us to talk about the effects the move would have on the children as well as on each of us. We tried to cover it all. Elise finally agreed that in this case my need was greater than hers. I was more miserable than she was happy.

We finally reached the point where we were ready to work out all the details. This took some serious negotiation because there had to be something in it for Elise as well as for me. We came up with a plan. I would come back to the Boston area two days a week to work long hours each day seeing clients and Elise would be on her own with the kids those two days. This decision certainly had some negative aspects to it but they were more than balanced out by the positives for both of us that came from being able to spend five full days each week as a whole family. Elise realized there was another potential plus for her—experiencing the responsibilities and benefits of being on her own (we'd never been apart on any regular basis before) two days every week. And since she was writing daily then, she'd have more uninterrupted time to work. Another big positive for the whole family was that they would be spending all this extra time with a happier more relaxed husband and dad. We felt we had each won.

Arguing is fine but don't fight dirty and never pull the rug out.

Fueled by a desperate need to win an argument or by a deep fear of losing you may feel driven to try to win any way you can, forgetting that a defeated partner is a resentful partner and that resentment corrodes loving feelings. Learn to argue on behalf of your relationship and not against your partner. Focus on defining and resolving the issue at hand.

Don't let your anger serve as a provocation for digging up all your past grievances. In the heat of an argument it's so easy to bring up extraneous problems that also bug you. Soon that little candy wrapper lying on the floor that started the argument is lost under an avalanche of trash. You might win the fight this way but you've left your partner feeling bad about themselves, you, and the relationship.

The dirtiest kind of fighting comes when you pull the rug right out from under your partner. The dust goes flying and your partner, thrown completely off guard, lands in a painful heap on the floor. A sure-fire way to pull out that rug is to push your partner's buttons. These are those sensitive spots that you know trigger upset or embarrassment for your partner. Knowing your loved one well has many advantages and some disadvantages especially when it comes to arguing. You may not know all your partner's susceptible buttons, but you know enough to do damage if you press any of them. This is especially true when you hit your partner's most vulnerable spots.

We all have those hypersensitive areas that we try to protect at all costs. There could be some kind of pain experienced in childhood, in a past love or work relationship, or something about ourselves that we may feel we have no control over like a phobia. Sometimes you discover a sensitive area quite by chance. But when you use that discovery as a weapon during some future argument, it will not only deeply hurt your partner it will negatively alter how they perceive you.

In the end it's not only about the outcome of an argument, it's about how you fought it. A clean fight is a winning fight.

Wipe up the mildew before it turns to toxic mold.

It is so easy to put things off for another time. You give yourself all kinds of reasons – timing is bad, you're too tired to tackle the task now, you have plenty of time to take care of it, you're waiting to feel inspired. The excuses can go on and on, from the mundane to the creative.

We all procrastinate although the tasks may be different. However, when it comes to maintaining good relationship practices it's important not to put off until tomorrow (or the week, month after that) what needs doing today.

This is not to discount the importance of good timing. But rather than wait for the good timing to magically occur, you need to make the effort to create the right time. So an issue comes up while you are out with friends and you or your partner do something annoying, insensitive, critical, hurtful. To have the argument at the moment the insult occurs – at the time you're with friends or acquaintances – would simply be adding insult to injury. But when you get home that night would be a good time to discuss what happened, argue it through, come to a resolution. Unfortunately, many couples come home, one storms off to the bedroom without a word (to let you know they're pissed as hell but are going to make you suffer by giving you the silent treatment) and the other pours a drink, reads a book, or, if equally pissed (either by the earlier issue or the current one) storms out of the house.

We've been told by many couples that this kind of behavior is typical for them and they rationalize it by saying that by the next day they had both cooled off. But when we asked if they dealt with the issue once they had calmed down, more often than not they say no, that they just let it go. Why start arguing when things were now better?

Were things better? No. These couples are deluding themselves.. Ignored upset or anger spreads like mildew. Leave it too long and that mildew could become toxic mold. Once that happens you are breathing in potential poison and serious measures will need to be taken.

Try to deal with issues and problems between you quickly and efficiently. It's as if you see that your partner left a wet towel lying on the bathroom floor and it pisses you off. If you ignore it or simply demand your partner pick it up and that doesn't happen, mold creeps in. Maybe you finally pick it up out of frustration only to see another wet towel on that floor a few days later. Nothing has been solved. Now there's more mildew.

Making a demand or ignoring a problem is not a hygienic solution. You need to work together to solve the problem in a positive, constructive way. Wipe away mildew and you'll protect your relationship from toxic mold build-up.

Express gratitude.

You come downstairs one morning and see that your partner has emptied the dishwasher. He's not only feeling proud of his contribution but wants you to appreciate his effort. Maybe you say nothing and maybe he thinks you didn't notice. So he points it out to you. You look at your partner and say, "What do you want—a gold star? I do this almost every morning. It's about time you pitched in a little." Want to bet tomorrow morning your dishwasher remains full? And that's not even getting into how your partner now feels.

Okay, maybe you're agreeing with this woman. Her husband should pitch in. We agree that partners should work together cooperatively whether it's housekeeping or keeping your relationship working effectively and happily. The question is, and one of the crucial points of our book is, how do you best go about achieving cooperation. Belittling and criticizing never garner positive responses. If anything, they make a bad mess worse.

We live in an environment filled with all kinds of tension and stress and they bleed into our relationships. Because of this, getting a reward for something you do is such a gift. Feeling rewarded decreases stress, lifts anxiety, gives true pleasure and happiness. In return it is important for you to express gratitude for these gifts verbally, demonstratively. In short, showing gratitude and receiving it are equal blessings.

Sadly, when it comes to intimate relationships expressing gratitude all to often is forgotten over time. You get lazy or too busy. Think about when you first moved into your new home. You gave it so much attention. You worked hard to get it clean. It was something new, something you took pride in, something you cherished. And being new, it was front and center in your mind. Then, as time passed, the newness wore off, you started paying less attention to how clean the house was, there were other more pressing items on your plate. So too is it easy to neglect expressions of gratitude to your loved ones even though you surely care about their happiness and want to relieve their stress. Not to mention that when one of you is less stressed and in a better mood it spills over onto you, onto your relationship.

On the surface, it seems like such an easy rule to follow. When your loved one does something nice for you, express your gratitude. Thanks, honey. That was so thoughtful. I'm touched. You're the best...

If you ask your partner if they feel you show them gratitude for their acts of kindness, many will say no. Why is it so much harder than it seems? Many reasons. You get to expect certain kindnesses from your loved one and take them for granted; you are too distracted or involved with other things to notice that a gift has been given; you get lazy or tell yourself your partner can read your mind and knows how pleased you are without you having to actually express it; you're annoyed at your partner for something not connected to their act of kindness and you can't separate out the two.

Expressing gratitude is essential for good relationship health. Every time you and/or your partner shows the other an act of kindness and that action is reciprocated by an expression of gratitude, your relationship is cleansed.

Focus on the good, not the bad.

When you tackle cleaning up your house, you will always be more successful at the task if you pay attention to each space you clean and appreciate the progress you are making rather than chastising yourself for not yet having gotten to other areas. Be happy with what you are accomplishing. Value your own efforts. This will help you to continue tackling the next messy spot and then the next. Keeping going and the space will ultimately be tidy as a pin.

Apply the same rule or principle with your loved one. If you invest yourself in an intimate relationship it's a given that you see both positives and negatives in your partner, just as they see both in you. The rule here is simple, focus on the good not the bad. Instead of finding faults, find the qualities about your partner that you cherish. That isn't to say ignore the bad, but if you invariably think of all the negatives about your partner you will give the negatives too much weight. And by so doing, you don't place enough weight on your partner's good qualities.

Sure, it's easy to lose sight of the good points when you are angry with your partner or when the two of you are in the throes of a fight. The problem is focusing on the negatives is like the clutter you haven't attended to. It's all you see. What a mess your partner has made.

I had a client who came in to see me with a laundry list of complaints about her partner. After listening to the diatribe I asked her with true curiosity why she was still in this relationship? The question gave her pause. She finally told me that her partner had many good qualities as well. When I asked her to name them, it took her a lot longer than it had to iterate the negatives, but after a faulty start it turned out she had a long list of positives to relate. I asked her how the good qualities stacked up against the bad ones? Which qualities did her partner show the most? She looked surprised. Obviously, she told me, she wouldn't be in the relationship if the good didn't outweigh the bad.

If your partner displays more good qualities that you value than bad qualities that are not so important, doesn't it make sense to spend more of your emotional time and energy focusing on those good qualities? Don't you want your partner to do the same? You have a choice. One choice leaves you feeling happier, more content, while the other choice has you in a state of disappointment and unhappiness.

Be more positive about yourself as well as about your partner. Negative self-feelings impact a relationship negatively as much as negative feelings about your mate. Own up to your negative feelings, ideas, and beliefs about yourself. Awareness makes you mindful of how these negative feelings have become a burden you don't want to carry. You can let them go. You can consider new positive beliefs and actions. Sure, we all have weaknesses and flaws. We're not saying it's easy not to make them front and center in your mind. It requires your willingness to be more compassionate and accepting of both yourself and your partner. With that acceptance will come great satisfaction and a sense of accomplishment.

Treasure each improvement.

If you and your partner are both successful at following our guidelines your intimate relationship will be much improved. Now, it's time to truly appreciate what you both have and treasure it. You have something well earned. You have something wonderful. You are no longer weighed down by unresolved feelings, endless hurts and disappointments. You know what the right thing to do is and have made a good start at best relational practices. You strive to show and receive kindness and understanding, you have experienced how compromise can make your relationship the winner. Your loved one is your top priority and you make sure they know this. And by working to carry out best practices you are providing positive leadership by example. You've both come a long way in the process of cleaning up your relationship.

Chapter Eight
Good Clean Fun

When you and your partner were dating an important ingredient in your falling in love was all the fun you were having together. Practically anything you did together was delightful—joining in on each other's interests, chatting about almost anything, eating out, taking a walk. The romantic movie was fun, as was playing sports together, reading on a rainy day, going clothes shopping, walking through almost any museum, running into each other's friends, were all fun. Not to mention the great joys of looking at each other, being sexual, traveling together. Having fun together seemed the natural order of things.

Unfortunately, nothing seems to kill the fun like a long term invested relationship. When the initial excitement has waned the fun together too readily fades away. In our professional experience we have found that many couples are unaware that fun mutual activities formed the bedrock of their romance, so it comes as no surprise that they were not feeling any inner pressure to keep up the fun. And a plethora of everyday busyness and mounting life challenges compound the drift away from fun together. There are fewer and fewer opportunities to embody the great reasons they fell for each other in the first place.

We've worked with couples that have come to live parallel lives when it comes to having fun. Joe has fun playing golf with his buddies and Anne goes off for fun girl weekends. Having fun with your buddies is great, but fun apart cannot replace the protective shine that fun together substantiates. Having fun together is fundamental to maintaining your sense of intimacy and connection.

As time passes it is too easy to lose the knack. Sure, when you were young lovers you had a great time hiking together for a weekend, but now, a myriad of reasons—can't spare the time, out of condition, plain old loss of interest—stop you from hiking together now.

Let's take Michelle and Gary who had the best times traveling all over the country on his motorcycle. Now they have children and Michelle insists Gary sell the bike because she thinks a Dad should not take such risks. Once Gary reluctantly agrees it seems to both of them that some of the air has gone out of their relationship. In my office they express their mutual wish to feel close again. They bring up how lonely they were before they met and how close they felt almost as soon as they started seeing each other and how much fun they had doing things together. Gary admits he is resentful about having had to sell the bike even though he understands Michelle's concerns now that he is a father. Michelle confesses that she used to be very anxious riding on the bike but overcame her fears because she wanted to make Gary happy. By airing out their feelings and being willing to be more honest with each other, they were able to concentrate on the challenge of finding new ways to enjoy their time together.

It takes time to have fun together and in the move from dating time (endless) to lifetime (hurried, pressured, busy) running out of time becomes a huge enemy of fun—somebody in the family is sick, work is going great but more success means more work to do, so it takes more time, and there's work around the house or apartment and chores that need doing; new and diverging interests take you away as can caring for aging parents, working on the car, responding to the needs of friends and, when you have them—the kids. And of course there is the unhygienic buildup of ill will that can leave you in no mood for any sort of fun with your ball and chain of a partner.

Elise worked with a couple that insisted they no longer shared any thing in common. The idea of having fun together seemed impossible. Jen loved movies, theater, museums. Rob found those activities either too boring, too expensive, or too tiring. He was a current events junky.

Watching CNN and MSNBC took up most of his time when he wasn't at work. On weekends, there was TV news and The New York Times. Jen could not see these activities as *fun*. If anything, she believed they made Rob more tense and edgy. Rob disagreed. This was invariably the start of Round One. The fight would usually go until there was a verbal knock-out, Jen usually the one down for the count. What had begun as an exploration of having fun together ended up—well, just as I've described.

In working with this couple, Elise suggested focusing on what made them happy with each other. Had they *ever* had fun together? Had they *ever* shared an interest or activity in common? Examining their dating behavior and what they used to enjoy doing together, they agreed they once liked going dancing. Rob was quick to interject that dancing was out now. *Bad knees.* Jen, however, reminded her husband that it wasn't only the dancing they enjoyed when they went clubbing. It was also the music. They used to love jazz. And now? They sort of forgot they liked that. They forgot the fun they used to have finding a club that was featuring a particular singer or group they had come to like. It had been years since they'd done anything like that. Rob was not enthusiastic about taking his wife to a jazz club and because of his less than positive response Jen at first felt it wasn't worth it. Why do something together if they're both not really into it?

Remember, people are often not enthusiastic about trying something new, or revisiting something they haven't done for a long time. It's okay. Start with a small step in the right direction. The activity itself can often change the attitude. As it turned out Jen and Rob did have a date night at a local jazz club. Rob ended up enjoying it thoroughly. He even came home the next evening with a CD of the combo they had heard. After putting the kids to bed they sat together of the sofa and listened to the music. One evening of fun became two. It was a start. Making or re-making the connection allows you to build upon it.

Several years back Elise and I were invited to a "game night" party. When we got there we found several card tables set up in the living room each with 4-6 chairs. About 20 people were milling about, chatting, drinking, checking out the tables. Each table was set up with a different game—Monopoly, Risk, Clue, and Trivial Pursuit. People were asked to choose a table and everyone settled in for an evening of game playing. It was something most of us hadn't done since we were kids. We'd forgotten how much fun it was. Before we left at the end of the evening we complimented our hosts for coming up with such a clever idea. It turned out that they'd both felt the fun had gone out of their relationship and they struggled to find something they might enjoy doing together. After a lot of searching, they each wrote down things they used to do alone, or together, that was fun. Liz put down playing Monopoly with her parents when she was a kid. Mark was spurred to think of games he used to play with his parents and remembered playing Risk and Trivial Pursuit. Combining the idea of playing games together with a mutual desire to socialize more with friends, they came up with game night.

Games may not be your cup of tea but it's the idea that's important. Liz and Mark made a serious effort to address the problem and they were creative in their approach. Not only did this spike their fun quotient, they helped their friends up theirs as well.

The point of having fun again with your partner is to generate good will, to enjoy each others company. Ironically, having fun together over the years takes a modicum of work. But it's the best kind of work, with great potential to be engrossing and meaningful. Sure, you have to make special time, push yourselves a little—or a lot—put off some chores, make the effort to find that babysitter, and figure it into your budget. It is good for the health and happiness of your relationship.

You may think going to some dumb movie together is a waste of time and money. You insist that sitting in the same room watching TV is fun enough. You decide it's too cold, too hot, too whatever to venture out for a walk together. You may think back to the old days, reflect on the fun you used to have bowling, dancing, hiking, etc. and complain that the combined aches and pains of aging you now experience take those fun activities off the list.

We are not saying you must duplicate the activities themselves in order to revive the old days. Elise and I had our first date at a bowling alley. I was so enamored I actually rolled 3 strikes in a row. A personal best which "proved" that Elise brought out the best in me. She seemed duly impressed with my skills although later she told me she was more taken with my sexy velour shirt than my bowling strikes. Still we went bowling a lot in those early days and had a great time of it. Skip ahead a bunch of years, hoisting a bowling ball puts my back out, Elise has chronic leg pains—we haven't gone bowling in years. Now we feel happy visiting art museums together.

The point is we want you to make the effort to re-generate the happiness—not the specific activities—you shared when you used to have fun together. You know each other longer now, you know each other better, what seems like fun now can be different than what you used to think was fun. What's important is that you're having fun together and it doesn't matter what activity you choose.

The more often you have fun together, the better you will feel. Yes, you can over do it, take too much time from other responsibilities. What an amazingly great problem that would be to have to solve!

Put having fun into your weekly calendar. Schedule a special time each week just for the two of you. Don't get flooded with excuses. Even if it's an hour or two once a week make it happen. Go out for dinner together – it doesn't need to be an expensive restaurant. It can be your local coffee shop. And if you can't get a babysitter on the night you planned a dinner date, don't chalk off the fun time. Wait for the kids to go to sleep and make something special together for dinner and eat it by candlelight (soft music and not TV in the background, cell phones on mute.)

Take a walk, get some ice cream, sit on a bench and watch the sun set. Do whatever it is you think is fun for you together. Just do it, as the Nike ad so aptly puts it.

Chapter Nine
Sex - The mess you don't need to tidy up

$\mathcal{S}$ ex is not a neat, tidy activity. It's messy. But this is one time messiness is called for. Having sex will go a long way to keeping your relationship in good shape by lowering the pain of accumulated resentments, relieving frustration and fostering intimacy. On the other hand, people in sexually deprived relationships are at greater risk of looking elsewhere to meet their needs which sets the scene for painful, untidy complications and the possibility of bringing sexually transmitted diseases into the bed.

Perfectly normal individuals exhibit a wide variation of ideas and behaviors about sex. These range from no sex is good sex, to there is no such thing as too much sex. There are those who believe sex is mainly for making babies. On the other extreme are those that believe their partner exists to meet their every sexual whim. Then there is everything imaginable in-between.

Our take is simple. Some good sex can be a great benefit to long term loving intimacy. By good we mean sex that expresses some degree of passion and excitement. The sex that does the trick for a particular couple can be more or less intense, more or less frequent, even more or less thoroughly satisfying.

The absence of any good sex puts stress on other avenues of achieving and maintaining closeness. However, from the start we'd like to emphasize that we have met many happy couples that have chosen for their own good reasons to forgo sexual intimacy. They found other ways to feel close and connected. So, as we see it, some good sex can be the icing on the cake more than the cake itself. But, wow, that icing can be delicious.

More often than not couples seeking help have told Elise and I that their sex lives used to be so much better than they are now. The less shy ones reminisce about the hot sex they had when they were dating and when they were newlyweds and bemoan the loss of the passion and intensity they used to feel. Obviously, this is a special case of the not having fun together conundrum.

What happened to that passion? Where did it go?

Sexual challenges come into play sooner or later in most intimate relationships. All the usual suspects can get in the way of passion: no time, kids sick, too tired, too many worries, arguments, physical illness, chronic or acute pain—you name it. Trying to deal together with these problems can go a long towards generating more positive emotions including sexual feelings.

We can't count the times women in treatment have told us that in order to feel like having sex they need to feel a positive emotional connection with their partners. Just as frequently we've heard from men in treatment that having sex with their partners is precisely what makes them feel closer and more intimate. It becomes a real *Catch 22*. All the more difficult because you never want to be made to do something you feel bad about. We need to find ways to replace refusal or concession with its boatload of resentment and bitterness, with compassion, generosity and the warming spirit of gift giving.

He's been irritable and inattentive but still wants sex that night. You are not feeling ill but definitely not in the romantic mood. But maybe you sense that turning him down right now would only make things worse. Your predicament is that you'll feel ashamed of yourself and resentful if you just let him have his way with you. You are most emphatically not his whore. Maybe you can combine protecting your self-respect with the spirit of generosity by suggesting that a modest conversation aimed at clearing the air would get you more in the mood. Here is a perfect example where each partner has to give a little to get a lot.

It's also important to pay attention to underlying issues that may be interfering with good sex. Are you or your partner repressing seriously angry feelings only for them to leak out anyway, making the sex less than fully satisfying or making you not want to have sex at all? We encourage you, when possible, to take the time to sweep out any crumbs collecting on your sheets before you get into bed. After all, who wants to make love in a crumb-filled bed?

Couples are not always on the same page when it comes to how they feel about sex. There can even be differences in how each person defines the word sex. From our point of view sharing physical pleasure when mixed with emotional pleasure equates to good relationship sex. There are individuals who get hung up on considering intercourse as the only real sex. Even if you define sex as reaching climax, there are many intimate techniques for giving and receiving the pleasure that will bring you to climax. Sexual intercourse is just one of the paths to a rewarding sexual relationship.

Although it can be helpful, even productive for couples to talk about their sexual relationship, they often find it hard to do, especially when it comes to sharing preferences. If they never say what they want they won't risk the embarrassing revelation of their secret desires or needs and they don't risk the pain and disappointment of rejection. But, as I often say to my clients, friends, and members of my family, the only chance of success comes with the willingness to take risks.

It will help get the conversation going by picking the best times, understanding that sharing is an ongoing process, and trying to be as open and honest as you feel you can be. This sharing will be easier if it comes on the heels of having created a more caring, trusting and loving connection with your partner in general.

What if you don't feel sexually appealing? You're too fat, too skinny, too flat chested, too hippy, too ... something. You focus more on worrying that your partner is judging you than you are on any pleasure your partner may be endeavoring to give you. Being self-critical, especially about your physical appearance gets in the way of sexual enjoyment. It can also be a problem if you are judging your partner's physical attributes or lack thereof. In either case, judging is a sexual turn-off. There is everything to gain by focusing on the positive qualities about yourself and your partner. If you are more optimistic, kinder, more generous, more accepting you open yourself to more joy.

Do not force yourself to have sex. If capitulating to sex is tantamount to enduring punishment it will just make things worse. Permitting yourself to feel abused is never good for your health relationally or personally. Your smart move here is to seek help from a Licensed Sex Therapist. Eliminate all the problems you can on your own and solve the remainder together.

The more infrequent sexual contact is between a couple the more it can become one of those issues that can easily slip under the rug. You think if you don't lift up the rug or you tiptoe around it the issue will lay dormant. We have found that when a couple incorporates a comfortable amount of sexual activity into their lives, the dirt dissolves. Routine encourages more routine. The frequency itself isn't nearly as important as knowing it's a regular part of your lives together, a part that is enjoyable to each of you.

What can you do to improve your sexual intimacy?

Get over yourself/your partner. You do not have to be beautiful to have beautiful sex. You do not have to be young or in tip-top shape to give or receive sexual pleasure.

Make a date for sex. Anticipation can stimulate arousal, desire, excitement.

Get in the mood. Watch a romantic or erotic movie together. Switch the time—if you've always had sex at night, try it in the morning. Maybe take a shower together first. If there are children, make sure they're being attended to (at school, at a friend's home, asleep).

Create a romantic atmosphere. Dim lights, candles, incense, make the room clean and tidy. Play music that puts you in the mood.

Be willing. If you have aches and pains, figure out a more accommodating way to give and receive sexual pleasure rather than to decline it altogether. Distraction is a great way of taking your mind off physical pain. If an argument is keeping you from wanting sex, resolve the argument or agree to discuss it at a later time.

Focus your attentions on your partner.

Be open. Say what you'd like. Ask what your partner would like.

Be daring. Respond to each other's desires with deeds as well as words.

Be inventive. Try something new. Do something you've secretly wanted to do but were too self-conscious

Be grateful. Treasure the moment and treasure what you are sharing together. Appreciate and value what your partner is capable of offering rather than focusing on everything you might want.

What are the don'ts if you desire sexual intimacy?

Don't abuse drugs and/or alcohol to get you in the mood. If you are intoxicated you will not be present. You will not be in the moment. You will not be able to give your best, possibly not give anything at all.

Don't use force. Forcing your partner to do something they don't want to do or feel ready to do is a surefire way to alienate them.

Don't bring up any stressful subjects before sex.

Don't bring a fight to bed.

Don't find fault.

Don't show disapproval or disappointment.

Don't be selfish. Don't put your needs thoughtlessly ahead of your partner's.

Don't forget about foreplay and afterglow. Try not to hurry through the experience.

Don't be judgmental, critical, deprecating in your thoughts or, especially, your behavior. You know better, of course, but these turn offs can slip out.

A word about make-up sex: There are people who unconsciously pick fights in order to end up having sex. A fierce argument can rev up explosive sexual passion. If the fight gets resolved first and then you have great sex, the altercation might be worth it. Beware, though, the bad habit of repeatedly bringing your relationship to the brink of explosive dissolution as your main way of ending up feeling close. It's akin to making a gigantic dirty mess so you'll feel so great after you clean the place up. You risk going too far and getting buried under your garbage.

We want to emphasize that it is never too late to clean up your act when it comes to your sexual relationship. Keep in mind that the longer you have gone without, the more overwhelming and awkward it is to get started again. Amazingly similar to the reality of house cleaning. And similarly the best practice is starting over with small steps. Begin with mindfulness. Listen, learn, connect. There is great free fun to be shared. The process of cleaning up your sexual activity creates healthy by-products. You'll sleep better, you'll feel more content, and your relationship will take on a kinder tone. A modest amount of not so clean sex can make your entire relationship clean up job more approachable and appealing.

Chapter Ten
The Sweet Smell of a Good Relationship

Most of us were taught by our parents to know the difference between right and wrong. School tried to teach us the rest. Yet few were taught very much about achieving and sustaining intimacy. Or, for that matter, how not to mess it up. Elise and I set out in these pages to fill in that gap with our views of the best and worst relationship practices. Engaging in good cleanup practices, whether they be personal bodily habits, taking proper care of your home and work environment, or behaving in caring, loving ways in your intimate relationships, all require getting rid of any old unhygienic habits and learning then practicing good habits that bring satisfaction and pleasure. We certainly believe that cleaning up your intimate relationships will bring you and your partner closer and more happily together.

Hopefully you have begun taking some relationship cleanup steps to clean and neaten your approach to each other and are already feeling that your relationship is more intimate and more sustainable now. What remains to be accomplished is doing more of the same as often as you can. The realities of life will fight you on this quest to keep your relationship in tip-top shape. What seems so obvious can easily slip away. You might consider rereading the book together now and again. Or try some of the steps you didn't try before and now feel ready to attempt. Every positive act will increase the stress hardiness of your love.

The lessons from the second half of this book—the what NOT to do list—are more challenging in some ways because they are mostly counter intuitive. Some little devil in us tricks us into making the mess worse just when we're trying to clean things up. The fewer you resort to the easier it will be to feel the love you are protecting with the positive steps.

Please be aware that the temptation to fall back on bad habits is everlasting. Whenever a conversation about some conflict with your partner is going awry it pays to figure out if you are letting yourself get trapped in a self-defeating strategy. When you understand what you are doing wrong start the discussion again. Expect that you will always be cleaning up false starts just as you never stop taking care of your personal hygiene or keeping your home free of clutter and grime.

One of our major take home messages is to minimize the creation and maintenance of grudges. By forming and holding on to grudges you make it difficult if not impossible to be happy with your partner. If you hope to stay loving you must let the bad feelings go as soon after they take hold as you can. They are your bad feelings, you can chose to throw them out and still work positively on the actual problem. The positive feelings engendered when you and your partner clean up your clutter—grudges, judgments, indifference, lack of involvement, dirty fighting and such—will make your efforts pay off big time.

If your relationship began with a period of being madly in love you have practiced many of the positive steps we've recommended without realizing you were doing anything so significant. Most couples slack off the infatuation driven good behaviors as the realities of life wear them down. You don't have to give into what you feel is unsatisfactory. Now you know there are steps you can take to bring back the intimacy. In fact, that intimacy will be stronger and more relevant because you know each other longer and better.

As your intimacy deepens you will experience a steady flow of positive energy. Where negative energy drains you and leaves you feeling separate, sad, and hurt, positive energy allows you to feel better about yourself and your loved one. The more you achieve the ability to forgive and practice mindfulness about what you say and do, the stronger will be your bond. When you are vigilant about attending to stress before it drags you down you will feel better mentally and physically. Incorporating more time for fun and sex with the freedom to define those terms in ways that meet your needs as a couple will bring added joy and closeness.

While you may sometimes feel challenged to follow healthy relationship practices the benefits you receive are worth it. Through the act of giving to your intimate partner you maximize your chances of getting good things back. That's how it works. And if that doesn't happen you may need to re-evaluate the relationship you've chosen to be in. Is it truly right for you? Don't accept the status quo if it is not working for you even after you've done all you can to improve the relationship. Seek professional help if you need it.

We hope you will take good relationship cleanup to heart and start putting your relational life in order. The practice of good relationship cleanup will lead to a successful partnership, one in which you are truly working to care for, help, and love one another. In a loving partnership you will feel a sense of wholeness, completeness, connectedness. The more you practice good relationship cleanup the more you will feel fueled to continue to practice it.

The goal is simple—to achieve an intimate loving relationship that smells so sweet and shines so bright it sparkles!

Appendix

When your relationship is clean and neat you get to enjoy being:

Partners
Lovers
Confidants
Pals
Playmates
Supporters
Fans
Second brains
Co-conspirators
Teammates
Backers
Comrades
Soulmates

You are a relationship cleanup champion each time you show your partner:

Tolerance
Appreciation
Enjoyment
Respect
Generosity
Fair-play
Devotion

Delight
Lust
Sympathy
Compassion

You are messing up your intimacy when you are:

Contemptuous
Raging
Cold
Dismissive
Cruel
Relentless
Superior
Intolerant
Unappreciative
Unapproving
Argumentative
Judgemental
Dismissive
Harsh
Rigid
Manipulative
Controlling
Revengeful
Scowling
Insulting
Ghosting

Authors' Note:

We encourage you to send any comments and suggestions that come to you as you read this book. There are so many ideas and approaches that we're certain we've missed or not delved into enough. We would love to be constantly adding and expanding our book. We will also be using the concepts we've developed here (and others that you send us) for our relationship coaching workshops with couples that want to work with us directly to clean up their act.

Find us on: https://www.linkedin.com/in/dr-jeffrey-title-07b120137/
Email us at: drjeffreytitle@gmail.com
Visit us at our website: www.drjeffreytitle@gmail.com

About the Authors

Dr. Jeffrey Title, Ed.D.

Bachelor's degree in Psychology, The City College of NY

Doctoral degree in clinical counseling, Boston University

Jeff received his B.A. in Psychology from The City College of N.Y. and his Doctoral degree in Clinical Counseling from Boston University. He worked as a clinical psychologist for the Massachusetts Department of Mental Health and was Clinical Director of the Massachusetts Department of Corrections—Reception Diagnostic Center. He then consulted on the founding of The Charles River Counseling Center and served as Director of Group Psychotherapy. He began an independent clinical practice serving couples and individuals in the 1980's. At the same time he created and ran on site consulting/mentoring for high-end technical sales companies and individuals. He developed a specialty in on-line and face-to-face mentoring of highly creative individuals in arts, sciences and business. He studied cognitive and spiritual approaches at the Mind-Body Medical Center, creating and overseeing professional communication email newsletter. He studied intensive couples intervention under Terrence Real at the Relational Life Institute where I achieved certification as RLT Master Therapist. He served as adjunct professor at Northeastern and Boston University and was on the Adjunct Medical Staff of Alice Peck Day Memorial Hospital in New Hampshire and at Fairview Hospital in MA. He is the co-author of Loving Smart: Putting your cards on the table, published by Warner Books. Relationship Cleanup: Keep the best, toss out the rest, is this second book co-authored with his wife. He and his wife will be running a relationship coaching program for couples based on their book.

Elise Title, M.S.W.

Elise is a graduate of The Bronx H.S. of Science, has a B.A. from Brooklyn College and received her M.S.W. in Clinical Social Work from the University of California at Berkeley. She worked for the MA. Department of Mental Health working as a therapist in the State's high and medium security prisons. Elise saw inmates for individual counseling and ran counseling groups for inmates.. After giving birth to their son she joined Jeff at the Charles River Counseling Center in Newton, MA. where she saw clients for individual therapy and ran several couples' groups. She then spent several years in private practice where she continued her clinical practice.

When she turned forty, Elise began her writing career and over the next twenty years published more than thirty novels—romances, mysteries, and thrillers. In addition, she and Jeff co-authored their first book on relationships, LOVING SMART—Putting your cards on the table, published by Warner Books.

Elise continues to write and, after having an angioplasty a year ago, has started coaching clients who have cardiac issues. She also began a cardio support group, Heartbeats, at her local hospital. Elise is looking forward to running a couples' coaching program with her husband based on their book <u>RELATIONSHIP CLEANUP.</u>

Work Sheets To Help You Get Started.

*G*etting started isn't easy even now that we've given you some cleanup tools.

It may feel confusing and a bit overwhelming to actually take the first steps on your cleanup project. To help you get started we've developed a pointed questionnaire.

You can make copies of this section so that you can each write out answers to the questions and then compare you answers, or if it suits your style, you can read each question and discuss your answers together.

When doing this task, it is imperative to uphold the principle of replacing contention with curiosity. To achieve a clean state of relational happiness it is more important to feel understood than to prove that you are right. And it is more important to achieve e a high level of understanding than a high level of good advice and judgment.

We want you to feel encouraged about this cleanup so let's focus of the positives that are already present.

1. What made you fall in love with your partner in the first place?

_____

_____

_____

_____

_____

2. What do you love about your partner?

_____

_____

_____

_____

_____

3. Which beliefs to you both share?

_____

_____

_____

_____

_____

4. What do you have in common?

_____

_____

_____

_____

_____

5. What do you agree about?

_____

_____

_____

_____

_____

6. What do you both like?

_____

_____

_____

_____

_____

7.   What do you both love?

_____

_____

_____

_____

_____

8.   What is your partner's most endearing trait?

_____

_____

_____

_____

_____

9.   What's the nicest thing about your marriage?

_____

_____

_____

_____

_____

10. What has been the greatest achievement of your intimate relationship?

_____

_____

_____

_____

_____

11. What was the most success you've had as a couple working out a problem?

_____

_____

_____

_____

_____

12. What do you have the most fun doing together?

_____

_____

_____

_____

_____

12. Do you share any tastes in common?

_____

_____

_____

_____

_____

13. What problem of your partner's do you feel most compassionate about?

_____

_____

_____

_____

_____

14. What is one thing you could do that would make your partner happy?

_____

_____

_____

_____

_____

15. What could you tell your partner that would help them understand you?

_____

_____

_____

_____

_____

Now that you are looking at your relationship through a more positive frame of reference it's time to tackle some of the mess.

1. Describe the moment you noticed your relationship starting to get messy?

_____

_____

_____

_____

_____

2. What beliefs do you and your partner disagree about that causes friction?

_____

_____

_____

_____

_____

3. What personality traits bother you about your partner?

_____

_____

_____

_____

_____

4. How do you and your partner's styles differ?

_____

_____

_____

_____

_____

5. How do your differing styles cause friction?

_____

_____

_____

_____

_____

6. Can you pick a grudge that you really want to clean up?

_____

_____

_____

_____

_____

7. When would be a good time for you and your partner to tackle this problem?

_____

_____

_____

_____

8. What would make it easier for you talk about a problem?

_____

_____

_____

_____

_____

9. What would make it easier to listen to each other?

_____

_____

_____

_____

_____

10. Are there particular issues you find it most difficult discussing?

_____

_____

_____

_____

_____

11. What would make it easier?

_____

_____

_____

_____

_____

12. Do you and your partner ever pose ultimatums? Give examples.

_____

_____

_____

_____

_____

13. If separating/divorcing is one of the ultimatums, what would be your greatest loss?

_____

_____

_____

_____

_____

14. Do the pros outweigh the cons in your relationship?

_____

_____

_____

_____

_____

15. Are you both willing to do what is needed to cleanup the relationship and not let it fall into disrepair?

_____

_____

_____

_____

_____

IF YOUR ANSWER TO THE FINAL QUESTION WAS YES, TURN TO YOUR PARTNER AND SHAKE ON IT!

Made in the USA
Middletown, DE
15 July 2019